painting with watercolours

Watercolour illustrations by Peter Wilks and Diana Morice

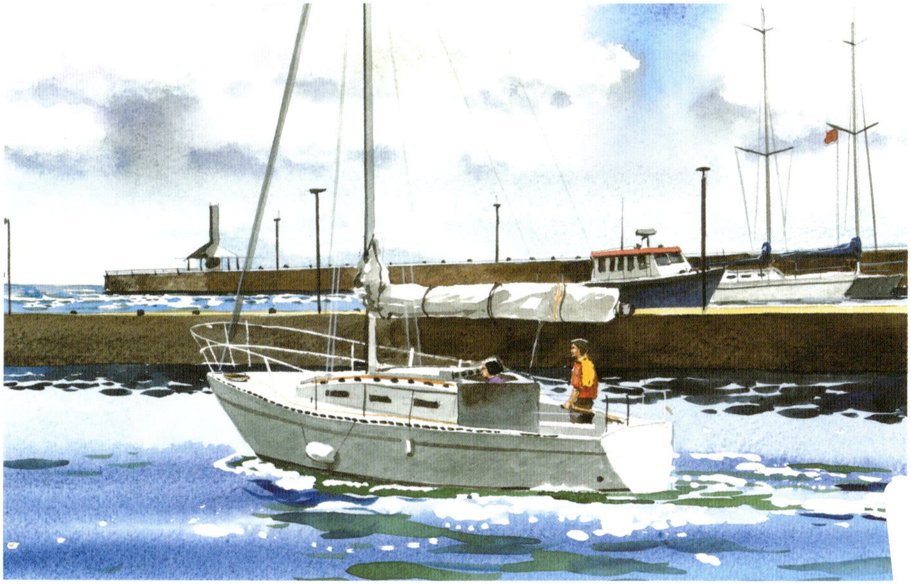

PUBLISHING PLC
Published by Top That! Publishing plc
Tide Mill Way, Woodbridge, Suffolk, IP12 1AP, UK
www.topthatpublishing.com

0 2 4 6 8 9 7 5 3 1
Printed and bound in China

Contents

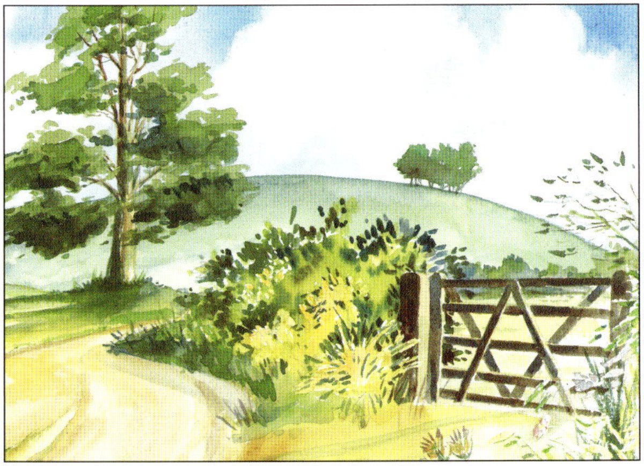

Introduction

The great thing about watercolour painting is that not only is it an accessible art form, it is a challenging one as well. While the serious artist will always find it testing, the novice will quickly be able to gain an impressive degree of competence. What is more, it is not a daunting hobby to take up as it is quick, clean and portable.

The translucent, light quality of watercolours can be used to create beautiful effects and help to make it one of the most expressive of art forms. Watercolour painting is also exciting because you can veer from loosely controlled strokes to intricate precision within the course of a single painting.

The first few pages of this book contain all you need to get the most out of your materials and should enable you to enjoy completing the projects which follow.

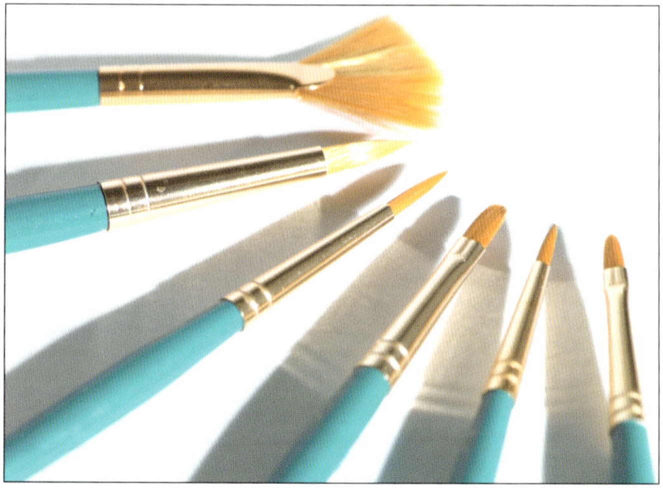

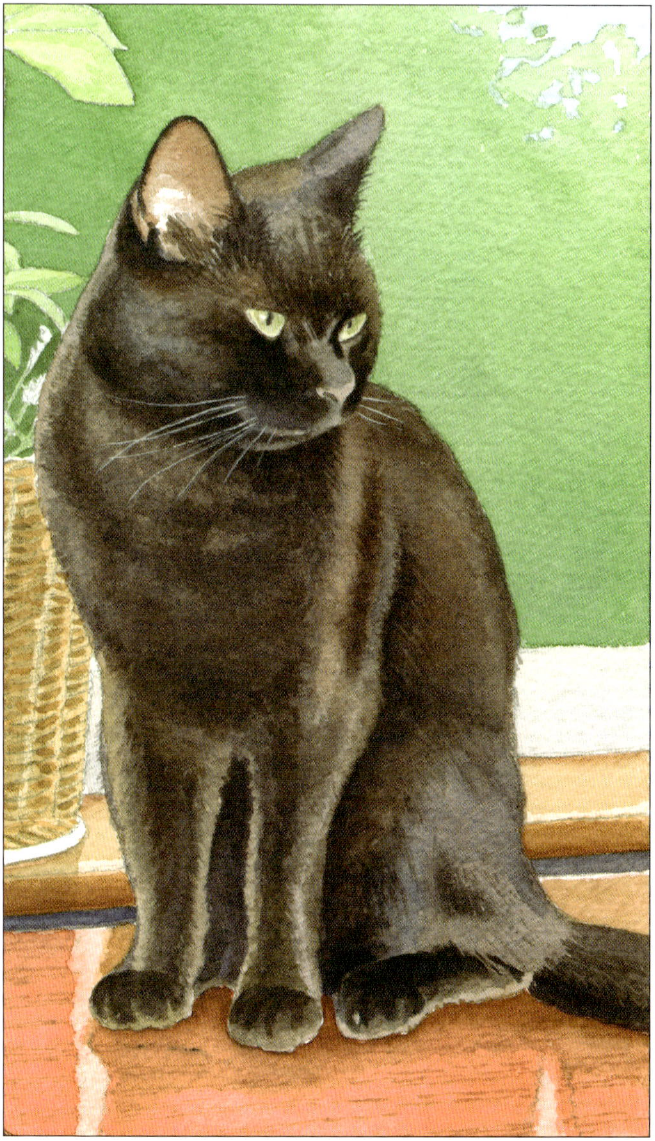

Materials and Equipment

The vital tools for watercolour painting are a sketchpad, paints, brushes, a water container, a mixing palette, a board, a pencil, watercolour paper, tissue and a putty eraser.

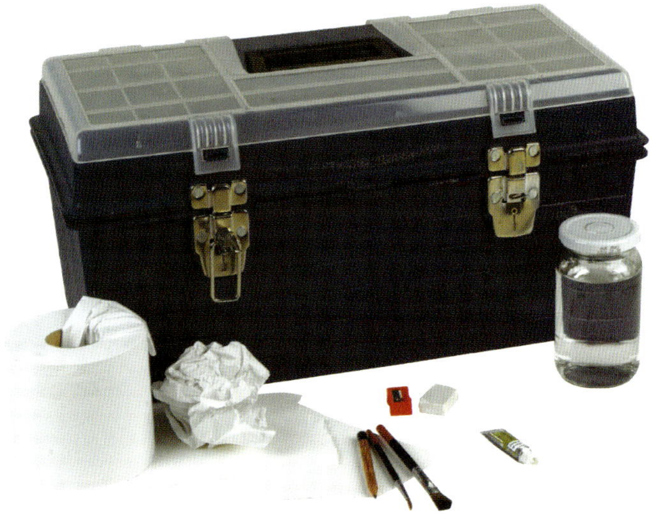

Paints

There are two types of watercolour paints available: student quality and artist quality. Student-quality paints are fine for the beginner and even the intermediate artist, but they do not have the same quality of pigment as required by the serious artist.

The paints are available in pans or tubes of varying sizes. Tubes are more convenient when painting large areas as they cause less wear to brushes and save time. Pans, which come in either small, square blocks or larger, rectangular blocks are smaller and easier to transport. There is no need to stick to a particular brand of paint as the paints should be compatible regardless of manufacturer.

Brushes

There is a wide variety of brushes available. The differences are in cost, the amount of water they hold, the ability to maintain a sharp point and the effects they create. There are round brushes, flat brushes, riggers for producing long fine lines, fan brushes for special effects and wash brushes for applying large areas of colour.

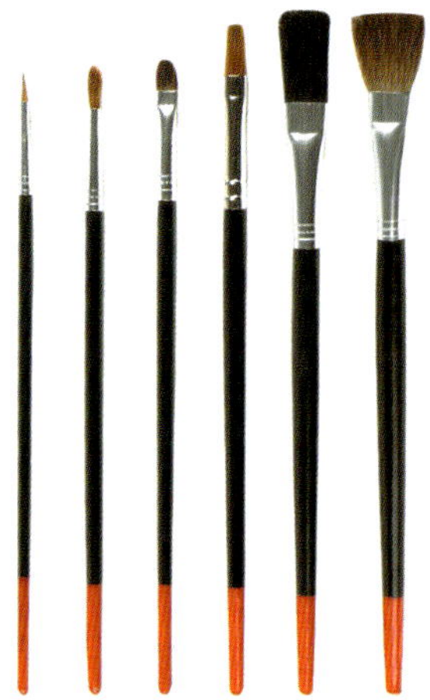

Unsurprisingly, perhaps, the best brushes will also be the most expensive. However, bear in mind that the beginner only needs a few brushes. Investment in sable brushes should also prove economically prudent in the long run – as long as the brushes are looked after – and will make it easier for you to establish a degree of control and spontaneity over your work.

Having said that, there are some fine quality synthetic brushes available that offer a realistic alternative to sable. They can last for a good length of time and are considerably cheaper.

Materials and Equipment

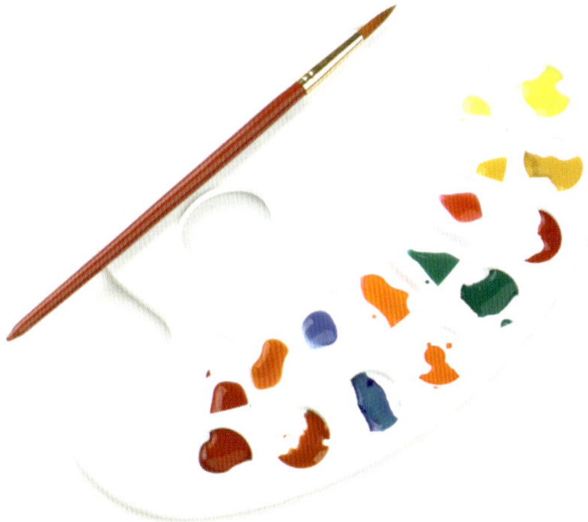

Mixing Palette

Palettes are available in metal, plastic and porcelain. It must be white, so that the colours can be seen clearly and it should have a number of mixing wells with sufficient depth to allow mixing of a number of separate washes. It is easier to gauge the intensity of colour in a flat-well palette than in a slanted-well palette. Many people use ordinary household plates.

Paper

It's worth investing in some good-quality watercolour paper once you have practised a lot and are comfortable with your paints. There are three types of paper available: hot-pressed, cold-pressed and rough.

Hot-pressed is good for paintings requiring fine control, cold-pressed is fine for most techniques and rough suits dry-brush techniques. Rough paper will also withstand a lot of wetting and scratching out.

You may find it beneficial to experiment with different papers to find out what suits you best but, when starting out, it makes sense to start with a standard 300 gsm paper.

It's worth noting that you may get away with not stretching thick stock paper and that the lighter grades are liable to bubble when wet.

Cartridge paper.

Watercolour paper. Good-quality watercolour paper has more texture than cartridge paper.

Materials and Equipment

Pencil

Use a soft pencil to lightly sketch out the composition of your subject before you begin to use your paints. With practice, you will be able to draw with your brush but, to begin with, it helps to work to a pencil-sketched piece, however vague.

Putty Eraser

Keep a soft eraser close at hand to rub out any visible lines once your paint has dried. Unlike a conventional eraser a putty eraser used gently will not damage paper unduly and will allow further paint application. Fashion the putty eraser into a fine point when you want to erase a small area.

Sketchpad

A sketchpad is immensely useful but only if used in a way that is effective. Ideally, you should do several sketches of your subject on your sketchpad, testing different designs and compositions, then progress to delicate sketches on watercolour paper before beginning to paint over the top of this fine pencil work.

Use the sketchpad to capture specific details of your composition, such as small objects and people, for reference.

Do not be tempted to skip the sketchpad section as this may have a detrimental effect on the quality of your work.

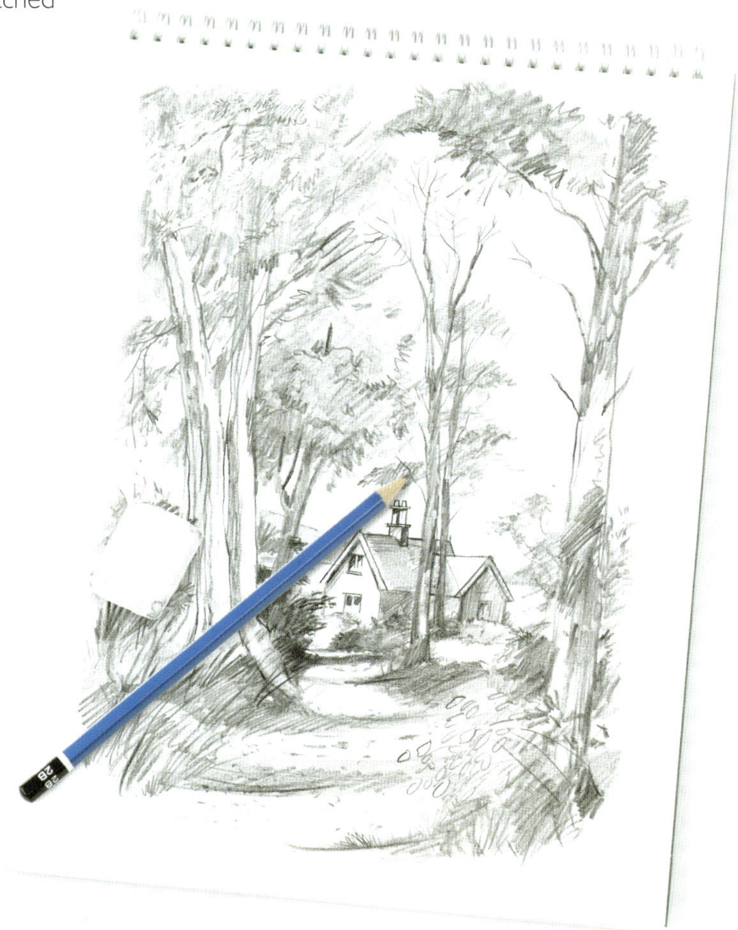

Setting Up

As with so many things in life, preparation is vital. The following list represents the best practice method:

Location

Before you begin painting scour your location carefully. You might be in an attractive spot, but the angle at which you paint your subject can make a big difference. When painting, look at your subject frequently, to see how shadow and light are affecting your work. Also, if painting still life, check that you have positioned the objects within your painting correctly.

Equipment

It may sound obvious, but before you start painting make sure you have all the tools you're going to need within easy reach.

Preparing the Surface

Always support your work with an improvised or shop-bought drawing board. Secure your sketching paper with masking tape, or for final pieces, stretch your watercolour paper.

Sketches

Do lots of pencil sketches first, building confidence in your skills. Your last sketch should be on the same paper you wish to paint on. Keep pencil lines soft and delicate.

Paint

Always mix more paint than you need. When applying washes make sure all your colours are ready mixed and keep the brush full and watery.

Water

Keep water to hand, in an old coffee or jam jar. Clean water will enable you to produce pure colour mixes. If painting on location outside you will need more water than can be contained in a jar so take a reserve supply.

Other Equipment

You will need some tissue or rag to hand, to lift off wrongly placed colour. Sponges can be used for creating textures and wetting areas. If painting outside in bright conditions, consider sporting a peaked hat. Sitting in the sun for hours can place a strain on your eyes.

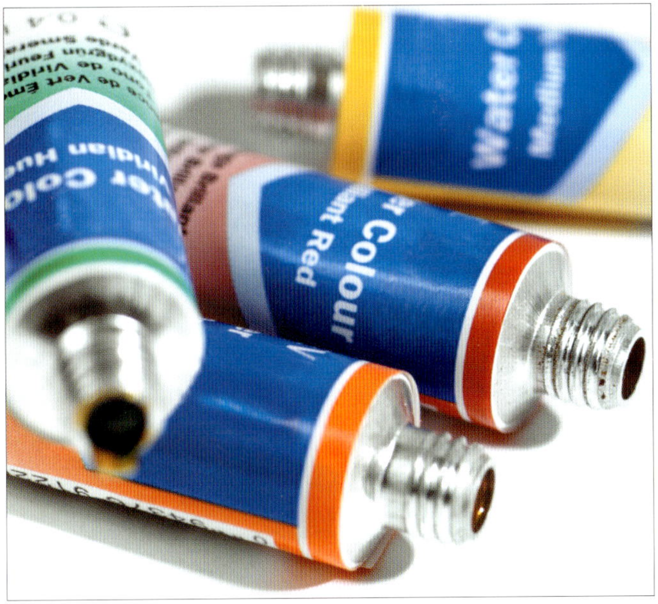

Basics

Stretching Paper

Watercolour paper should be stretched prior to painting to prevent it cockling (wrinkling and bending). Wet the paper, then fasten the edges of the paper to a board with moistened paper tape (available from artists' shops). Leave to dry completely. The resulting paper is stretched like a drum.

How to Hold a Brush

Your hand should be comfortable when you paint, or your work will look strained and stiff. Hold your brush in the middle between your thumb and forefinger, and practise making a few strokes in the air before you load it with paint or water. If you want greater control over your brush – particularly useful when painting fine details – hold the brush a little nearer the bristles.

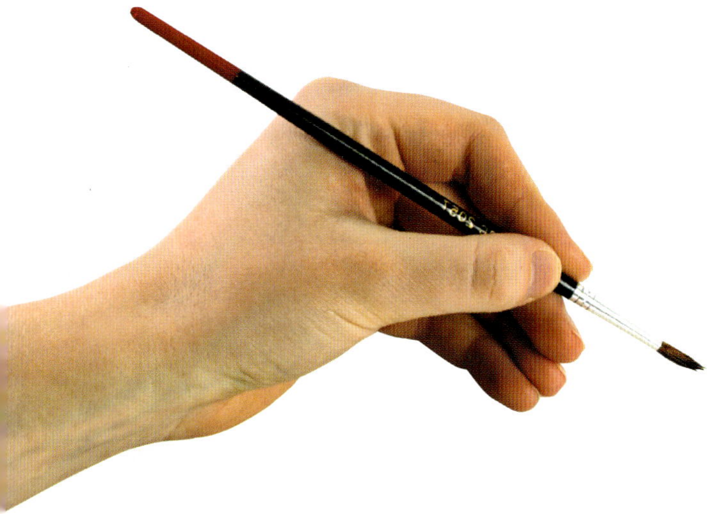

Warm to cool.

Cool to warm.

Cool and Warm Colours

Colours are divided into two groups: warm and cool. Red, orange and yellow are warm, blue and green are cool. Colours can be warmed up, or cooled down, by adding a little of a colour from the opposite group. The effect will depend on the proportion of each colour used.

Light and Shade

The more paint you use, the less light will be present within your picture. The purest colours are made by combining two primary colours. Nature, however, rarely produces these hues; light and shadow have the effect of brightening or dulling a colour. You can show this by using greys, browns and purples to represent areas of shadow and distinguishing highlights.

Mixing Palette

The colour block below shows you which colours you need to combine, with water, to create different shades of paint. Practise mixing on a palette before painting a picture. For large areas of colour, mix plenty of colour first, as it is hard to recreate an exact shade.

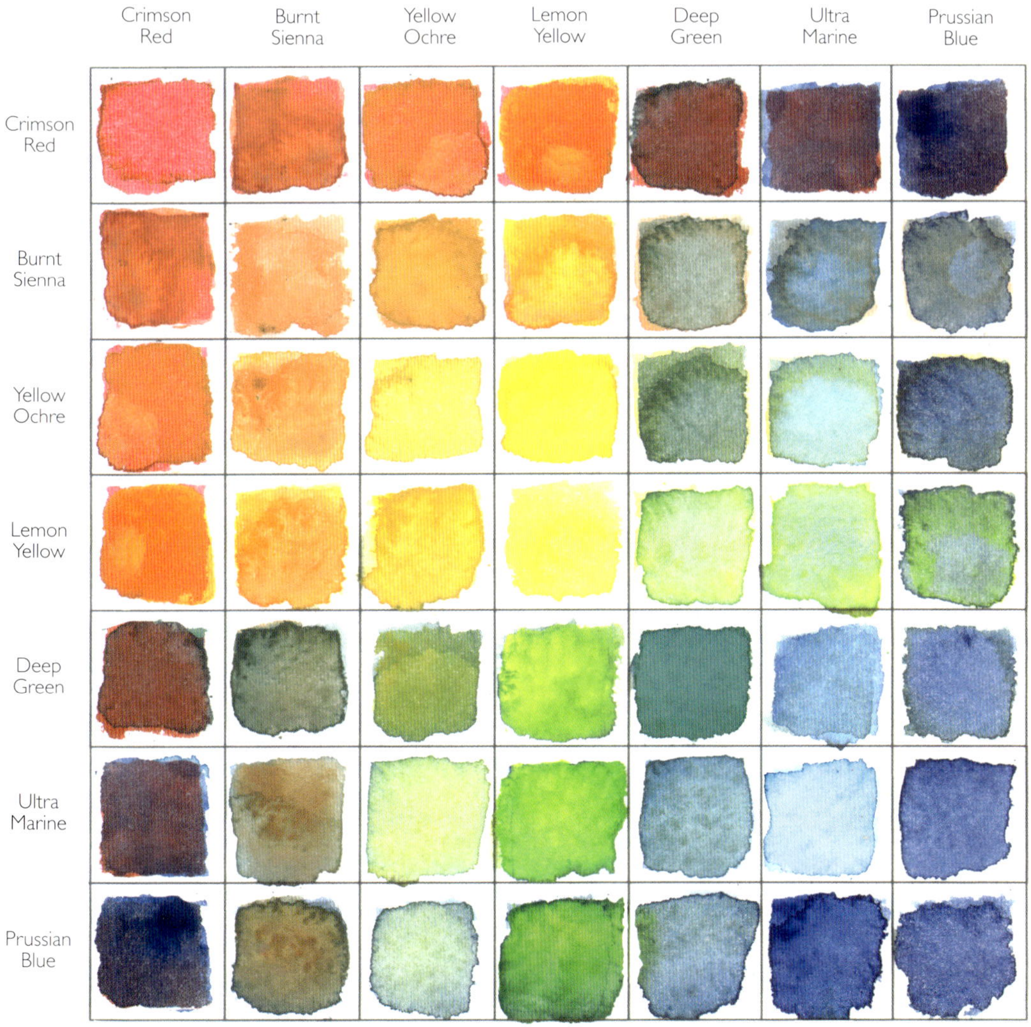

Washes

Flat Wash

A flat wash is simply a wash of the same colour tone. Use the biggest brush you can and keep a good mixture of paint and water ready. Paint from the top in horizontal, slightly zigzag strokes, keeping within marked boundaries outlined in pencil, and let each stroke settle before continuing. Remove excess fluid with the tip of a dry brush.

Flat wash.

Graduated Wash

A graduated, or graded wash, can be either a wash with changes in the intensity of colour, or a wash which changes from one colour to another. The two principle graduated washes are grading from dark to light and grading from one colour to another.

Graduated Wash.

Grading from Dark to Light

Start with full colour at the top and add more and more water as you move down the page. The effect is translucent and allows the texture of the paper to show through.

Grading from Dark to Light.

Washes

Grading from One Colour to Another

Instead of diluting the first paint colour, simply add more and more of the new colour. Mix the two different pigment solutions before you start, then make a broad stroke with one. Follow this with a blend of the two colours, and then finish with a brush dipped in only the second colour.

Grading from One Colour to Another.

Blended Wash

A blended wash begins in the graded manner. The brush is then rinsed, loaded with a contrasting colour and stroked across the top of the graded area, blending in with it.

Blended Wash.

Variegated Wash

A variegated wash is a wash of several different colours in either a deliberate or a haphazard way. The colours are allowed to bleed into each other. This wash can work particularly well when painting sunsets.

Variegated Wash.

Techniques

Solid Shading

Solid shading is used to create strong contrast between the light and dark areas of a picture. For this to be effective, you should use complementary colours in the lighter areas of the painting.

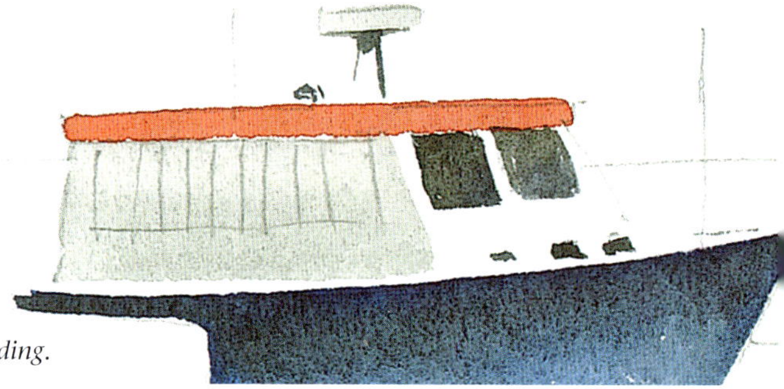

Solid shading.

Highlights

A small, soft ball of tissue can be used to blot wet washes into cloud shapes and add softly highlighted areas. The effect here has been achieved by gently dabbing a ball of tissue over long, thin areas of damp paint, removing the colour and leaving soft edges to look like clouds. In some places, a little paint has been allowed to remain, creating areas of highlight.

Highlights.

Hatching

Hatching is used to darken one side of an object, throwing it into shade. This effect is created by using lots of thin, closely-packed lines along the area in shadow. It's important not to overuse this technique as you may end up with a picture that looks laboured.

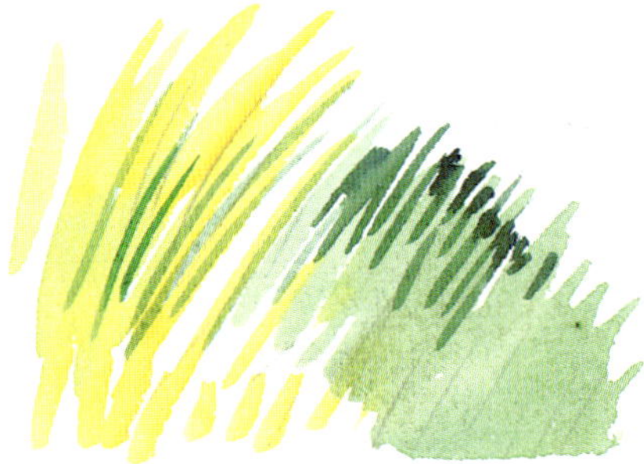

Hatching.

Techniques

Crosshatching

Crosshatching allows you to depict shadow on curves and rounded objects. This effect is created by criss-crossing lines to create an area of raised shadow. As with hatching, this technique should be used sparingly and only for special effect.

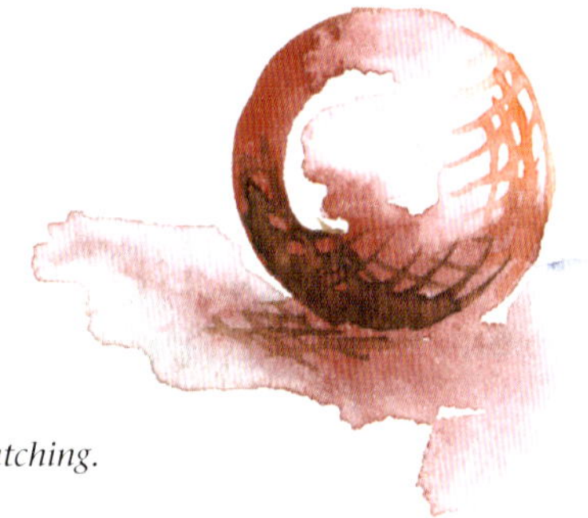

Crosshatching.

Wet-in-Wet

Wet-in-wet just means applying paint to wet paper or a colour which is still wet. The wet-in-wet technique can be applied over existing washes provided they are dry. Simply wet the paper with a large brush and paint into the dampness. The soft marks will work well in subtle background areas.

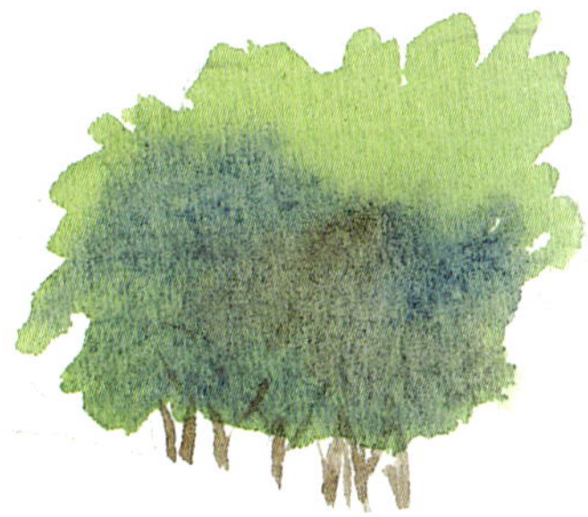

Wet-in-Wet.

Dry Brush

Load a brush with paint (and very little water) and drag it over bone-dry paper. The marks produced by this technique work best around a painting's focal point as they are crisp and hard edged. This is another technique to be used sparingly and with care.

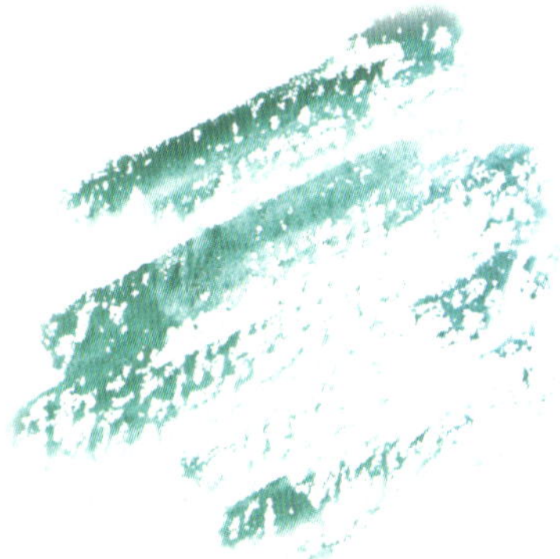

Dry Brush.

Techniques

Lift Out

This is a technique to remove colour from the paper to produce highlights. Paint an even wash on damp paper. Using a clean, dry brush or a tissue lift out some of the colour to reveal the whiteness of the paper.

Often this technique is used for skies to create soft, fluffy clouds by painting a graduation of blue and then lifting the colour back off with a tissue or a sponge. Timing is important. If the wash is still too wet then the colour will bleed back into the removed area, however if it is too dry it cannot be removed.

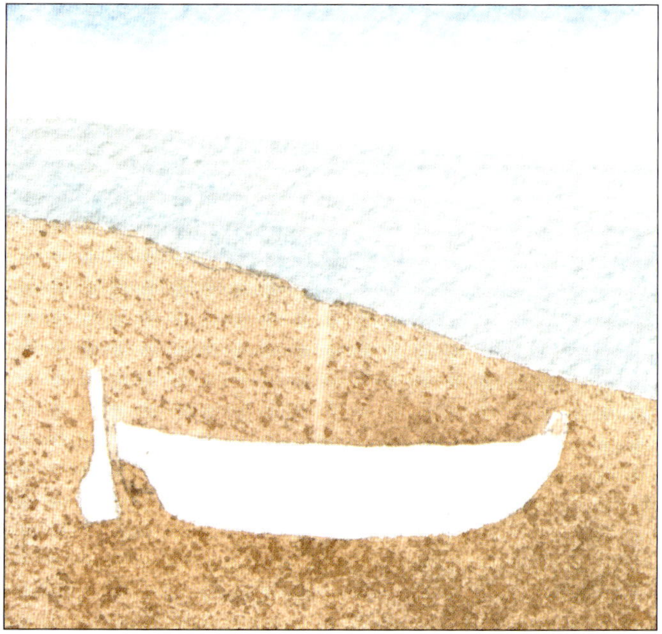

Spattering

Sometimes you want to depict a coarse, even texture, perhaps to depict shingle on a beach. A good way to do this is to spatter paint onto the surface of the paper or onto a wash.

Mix up a heavy load of colour, use a coarse brush or toothbrush with stiff bristles to dip into the colour. Then, either run your thumb through the bristles causing it to flick paint onto the surface, or knock the brush against your hand so that paint spatters onto the surface. You may wish to use masking fluid or card masks to protect some areas.

Granulation

A natural feature of some pigments is that they separate into grains producing an interesting, speckled texture. One such colour is cerulean blue. The effect also happens when painting a wet wash over a dry wash.

With your drawing board, flat paint a wash of cerulean blue, and watch the grains separate. Experiment with the wetness or even pre-wet the paper to see how this effect can be controlled. Information from paint manufacturers to identify which colours granulate should be available.

Scraping and Scratching

A variety of effects can be achieved by scraping or scratching to create highlights or texture. Do these at the end of your painting.

On a wet surface, scratch marks will darken as the paint is drawn into the damaged surface of the paper. On damp paper, the colour can be scraped off to either reveal the paper or to thin the colour. On dry paper, you can scratch and scrape back to the paper without any bleeding of the colour.

Techniques

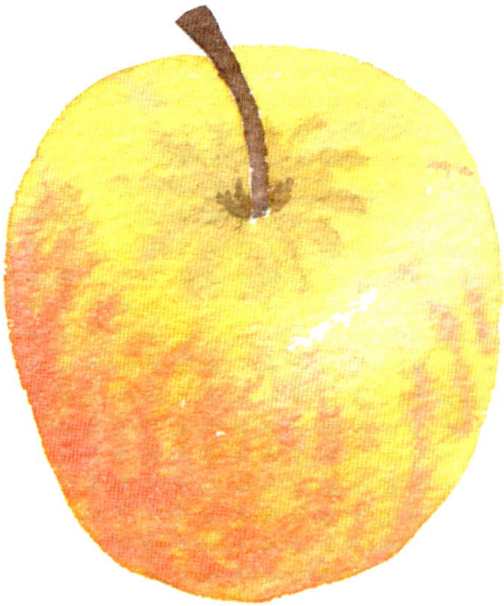

Edges

You can control the edges of your brush strokes by painting onto wet paper or by using a clean, wet brush.

Three different sets of lines are shown here. Hard lines are created by painting wet on dry paper. Soft lines are created by painting on slightly wet paper, where the edges soften as the paint bleeds. Broken lines are created by painting dry-on-dry, deliberately leaving a speckled broken line.

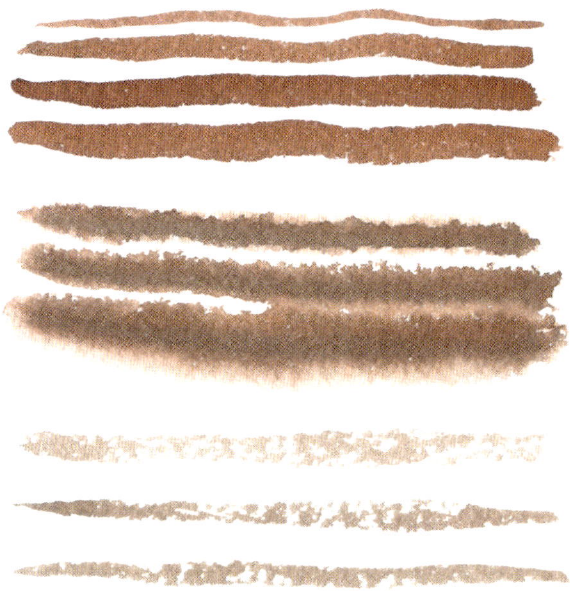

Dropping in Colour

Create a flat wash of colour, then, with the paper still wet, drop in other colours. You will have to consider the resultant effect.

With this apple, an overall yellow wash was applied first. While the paper was still wet, red and crimson were dropped onto the wash from the tip of a brush. The result is that the red runs into the yellow creating oranges and reds. Around the stalk a little dark ochre was dropped. The result is completely dependent upon the dampness of the paper.

Techniques

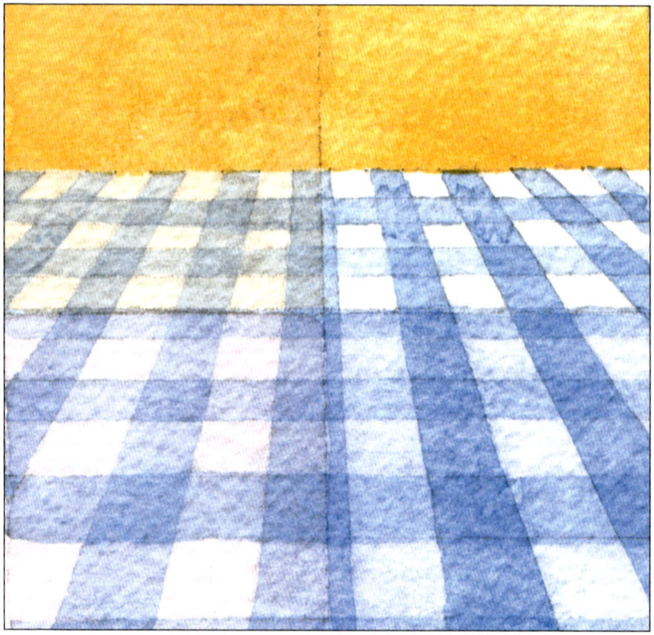

Using Masking Fluid

Use masking fluid to protect the surface from paint. Although masking fluid is not always easy to use. Apply the fluid with a brush or applicator to an area you wish to mask and allow it to dry. For thin lines draw out fluid from a pool using a tooth pick (as with the flowers here).

Wait for the fluid to dry before painting. When you want to expose the surface again, wait until the painting is dry and gently rub away the dry mask. The surface of some watercolour papers are too delicate for masking fluid, so do a small test first.

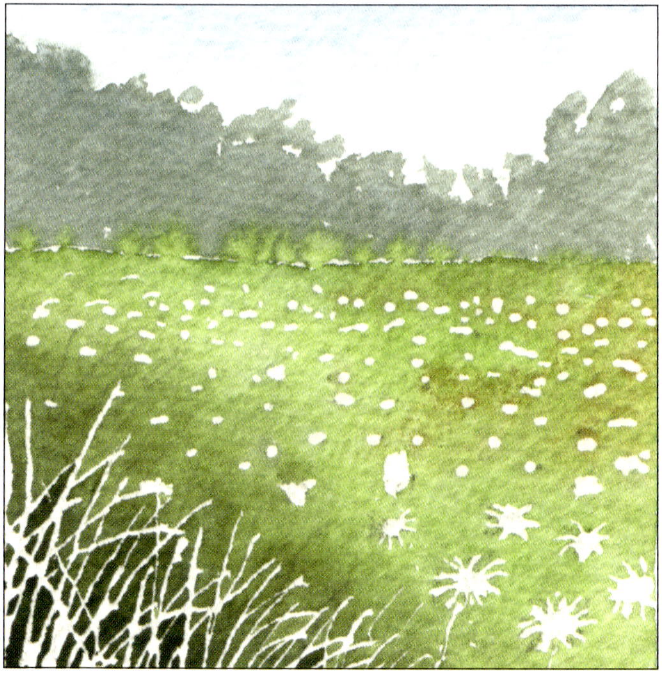

Layering

By over-painting a series of washes, colour can be built up or the tint can be changed.

Paint a simple background of ochre and a tablecloth made up by painting blue lines in one direction, then in another when the first blue lines are dry. Where the colours overlap, a stronger layered blue has been made. The top right quarter of this painting has been left like this but the top left quarter has had a thin wash of ochre, the bottom left a wash of crimson and bottom right of ultramarine. The four corners show even the lightest wash can alter the colour.

Textures

Salt
Scattering salt crystals into wet paint can make for some interesting effects. Lay down a wash, scatter the salt crystals, then leave the wash to dry completely before gently brushing the salt.

Salt.

Soap
Mixing paint with soap can create some interesting, if unpredictable, results. Soap will thicken paint without affecting its translucency.

Soap.

Sponge
Dabbing paint onto paper with sponges over washes creates great effects, but don't overdo it. Sponges can be used to suggest ripples on water and even for hair.

Sponge.

Textures

Stippling

Load a small amount of paint onto an old brush or sponge and then 'pounce', or dab, up and down on the paint surface. This will allow some of the background colour to show through, adding texture to your painting.

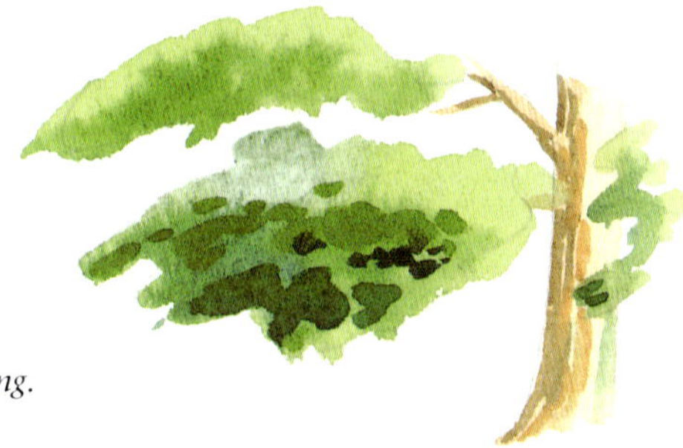

Stippling.

Toned Ground

A toned ground is simply a base colour which is flooded and allowed to dry. The painting is then painted on top of the base colour. This effect can be used to create a mood for a painting.

Toned Ground.

Line and Wash

Line and wash can be approached in two ways. Start with a line pen drawing (any water-soluble pen will do) and work water into and over the drawing. This can give very satisfactory results and, with the addition of a few colours, is a good way to start some projects. Alternatively, start with a watercolour wash and while it is still wet, draw into it with pen and ink. This will create some interesting effects but bear in mind that different inks will make for different effects.

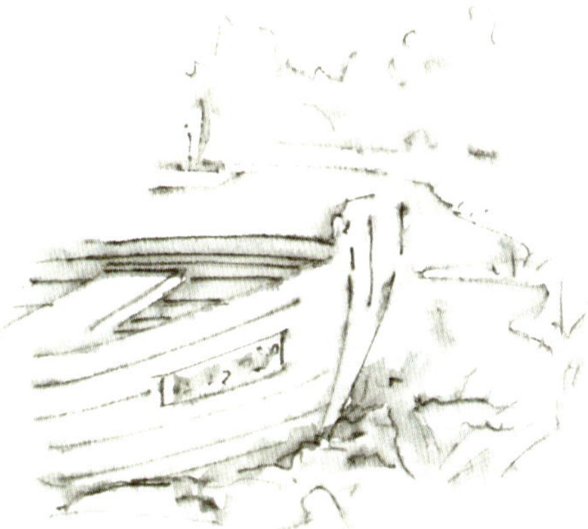

Line and Wash.

Composition

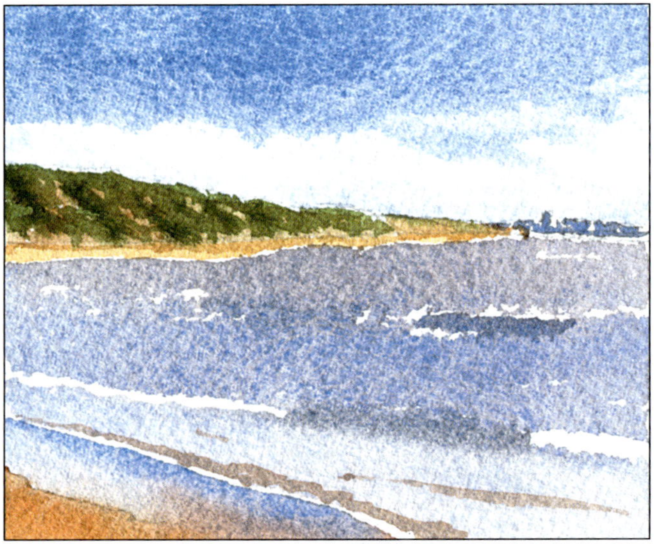

The top picture shows a headland with a town, grass covered cliffs, a sandy beach and sea. The composition is reasonably pleasing, but there are two natural lines that are breaking up the picture. These lines are the foot of the cliffs and the edge of the sea. The result of these lines is to cause the eye to have to jump from the foreground to the background.

The bottom picture is essentially the same view, but the natural lines now lead the eye from the foreground in an arc (by line and colour) to the headland in the background. There is also a better sense of space and distance because the viewer is able to walk the imaginary beach from the foreground to the background.

Often it is tempting to paint exactly what we see and not even consider the composition, but this misses an opportunity to improve your picture.

This is not to say that you must change things, but alteration should at least be taken into consideration. Sometimes, it's just a case of selecting the best part of a scene by using a viewfinder or making two 'L' shapes with your fingers. However, there will be times when you need to add something (maybe a figure or bird), move something for better balance, or to leave something out completely.

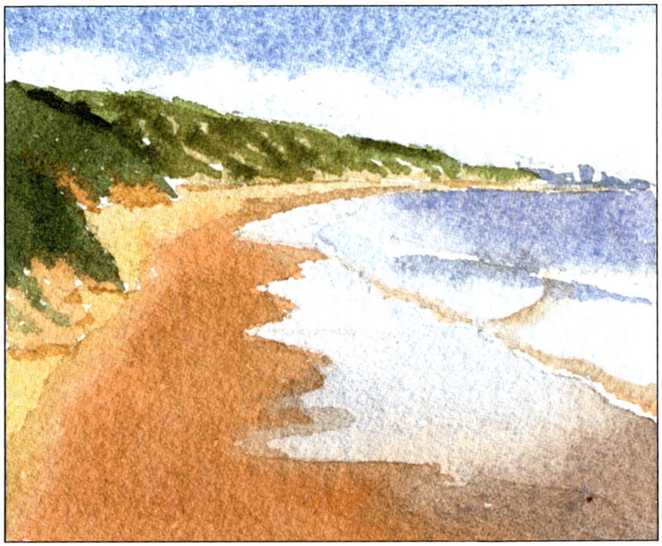

Composition

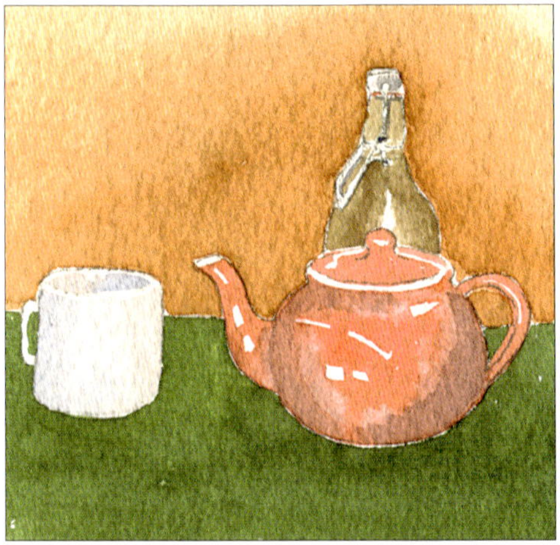

When constructing your composition, you must consider the focal point. This is where the eye is naturally led to. The focal point should be where the main subject of the painting is. We can help the eye reach the focal point by using features such as hedges, paths, fences or even ploughed field furrows.

There are many things to consider. Always use perspective, make sure there is a good balance, but avoid symmetry, selectively repeat shapes and emphasise light objects by placing something dark behind them. Remember that the eye cannot focus on everything at once so limit the detail. Lastly, try sketching several thumbnails to see how different compositions work. The top picture shows a simple composition of a bottle, teapot and mug on a green tablecloth. Nothing is really wrong here, except one object is half hidden behind another and the other object is a little isolated by itself. The tablecloth is uninteresting and it also cuts the picture in half. This would be even worse if it was not broken by the objects.

The bottom picture shows the same three objects, but with a few changes. The bottle is still behind the teapot, but its position is better defined because we can see part of its base. The mug is much closer to the other objects and the shape of the space between is more pleasing and balanced. The eye now easily flows along the tops of the objects. The tablecloth is angled to add a little more depth.

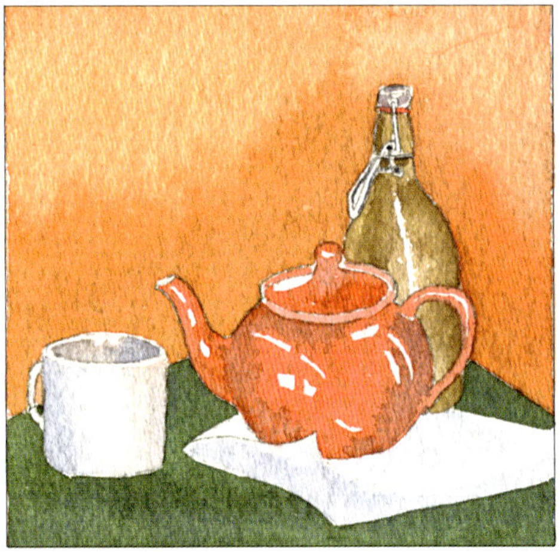

Perspective

The most important thing to remember is that figures appear smaller as they get further away from the viewer. Also, they usually become less detailed and softer in tone and colour.

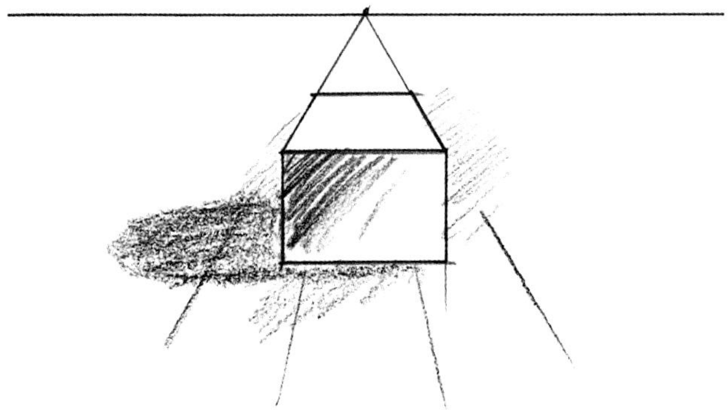

1. An object can be drawn with all the lines disappearing to one point – the vanishing point. The vanishing point sits on the horizon line – the line at which the sky and sea appear to meet.

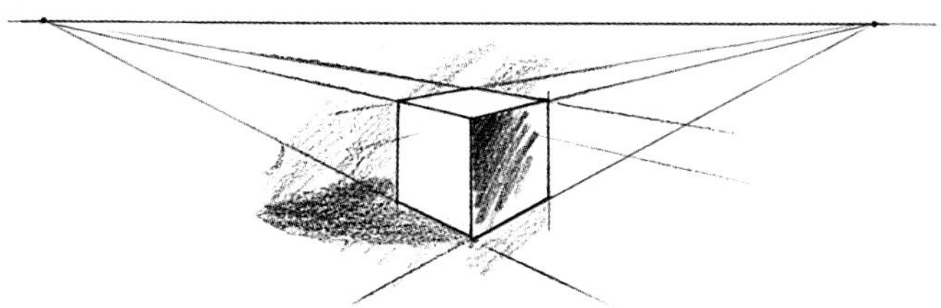

2. Here, the eye level is above the top of the object, so the object is looked down upon. The perspective lines disappear into two vanishing points.

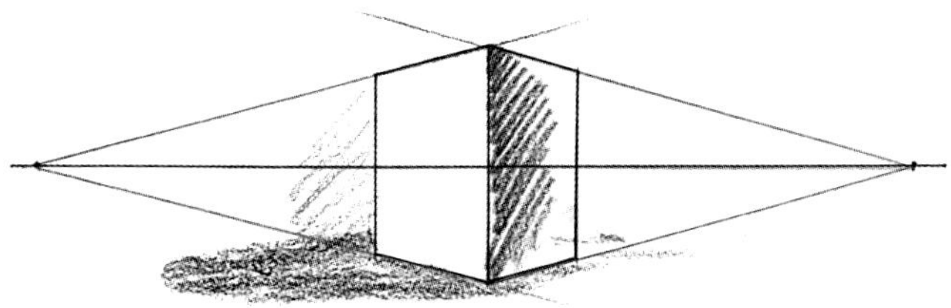

3. In this view, the eye level is near the middle of the object. Painting at this level creates the impression that the subject is at the same level as the artist.

Perspective

4. Here, the eye level is below the object. Bear in mind what response the angle at which the subject is painted may inspire in the viewer. The viewer will undoubtedly respond differently to two paintings of the same subject from different angles.

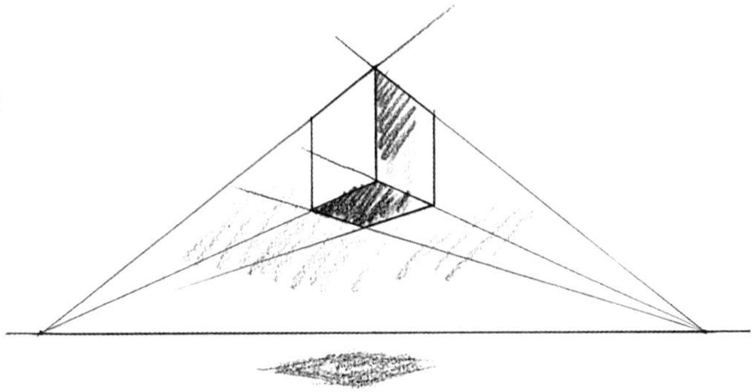

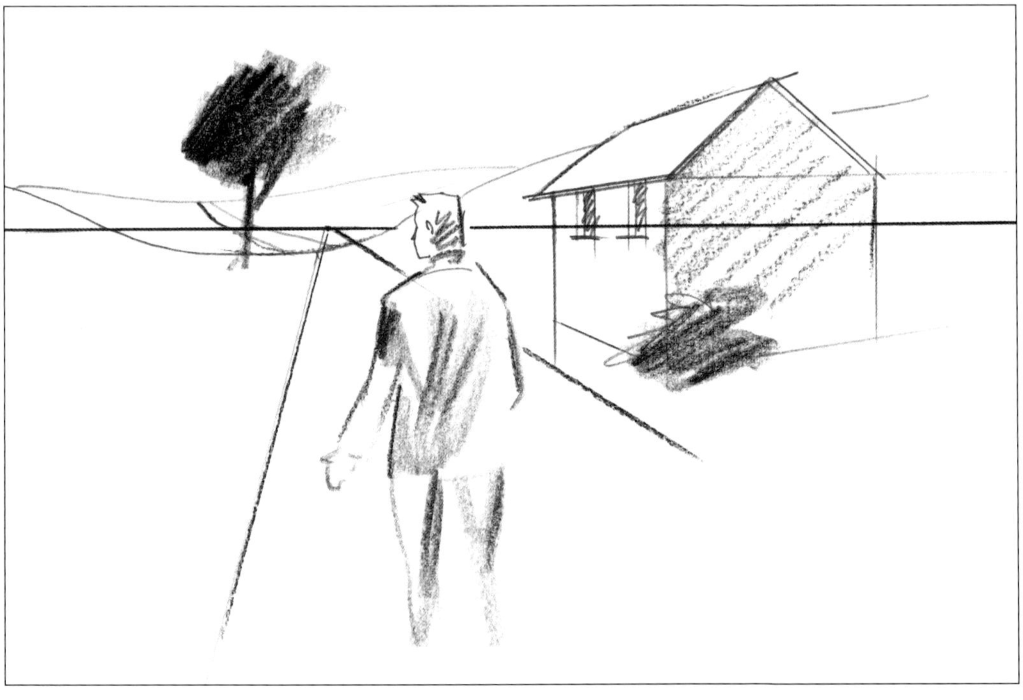

5. In this sketch, the viewer's eye level is at the same level as the figure in the picture. This creates an interesting effect, perhaps providing a sense of realism in the sketch.

Perspective

6. Add drama to tall buildings by using two vanishing points as before, but this time add a third vanishing point, for the building to disappear into. To help the effect, eye level should be at the base of the object being drawn. The angle at which you paint a building is particularly important. From a straight-on perspective, it will look flat and one-dimensional.

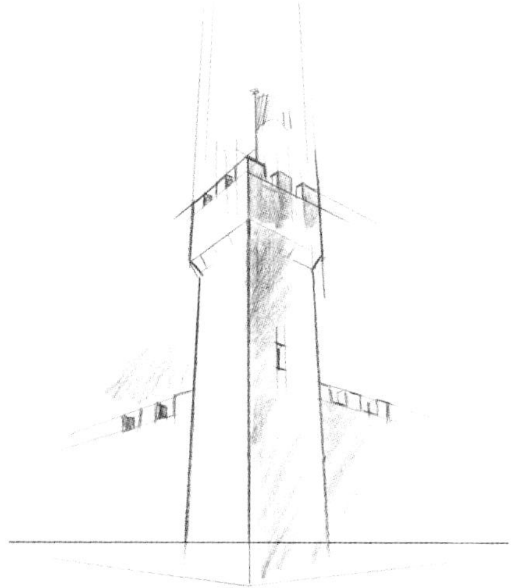

7. When drawing cylindrical or unusual shapes, using straight lines will ensure that you get it right. Here, two diagonal lines disappearing to two vanishing points establish the centre line in this perspective. An ellipse can then be drawn in the square.

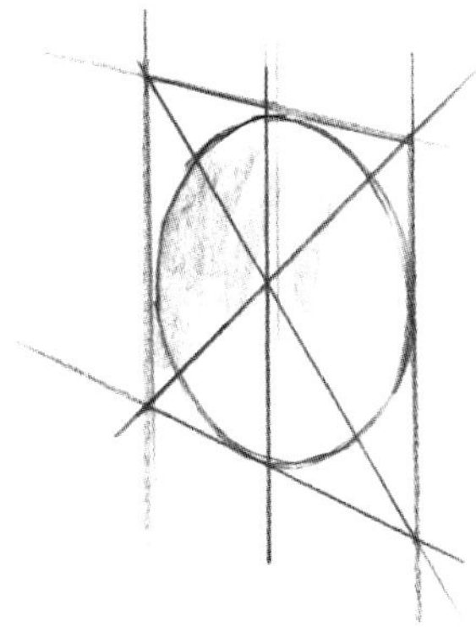

8. By establishing the first ellipse, you can then chart the position of the second. The ellipses effectively sit in a box. The lines of the box can be erased at a later stage.

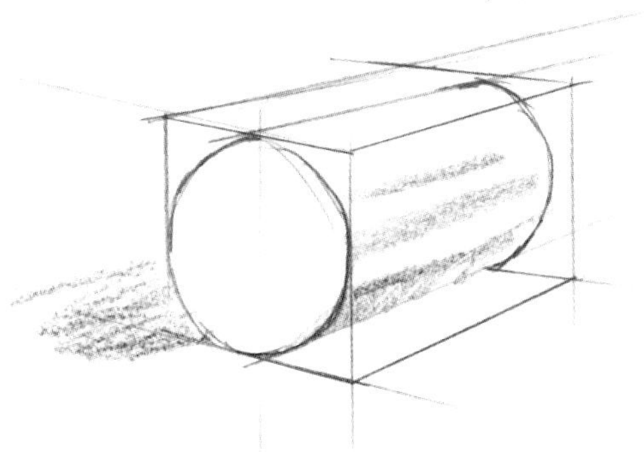

9. To draw a vase or similar object, draw ellipses in perspective around a centre line to make the shape symmetrical. The simplest way to draw an ellipse is to draw a rectangle first and then draw an ellipse touching the sides afterwards.

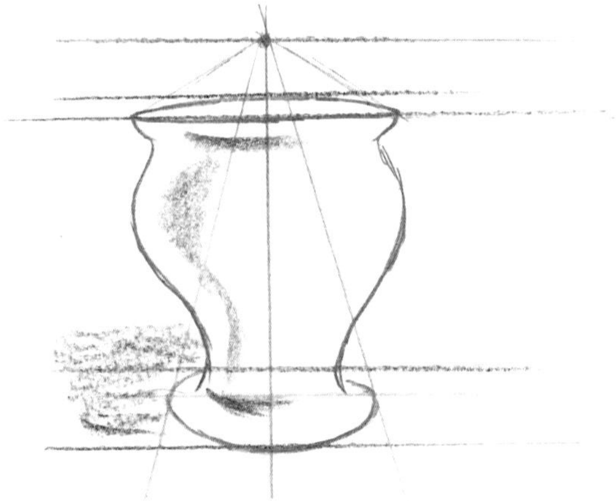

10. When you have mastered simple cylinders and vases, you can move onto more complex items, such as fishing boats. Once again, use a perspective box to help you draw the shape. The lines disappear in the same way as before.

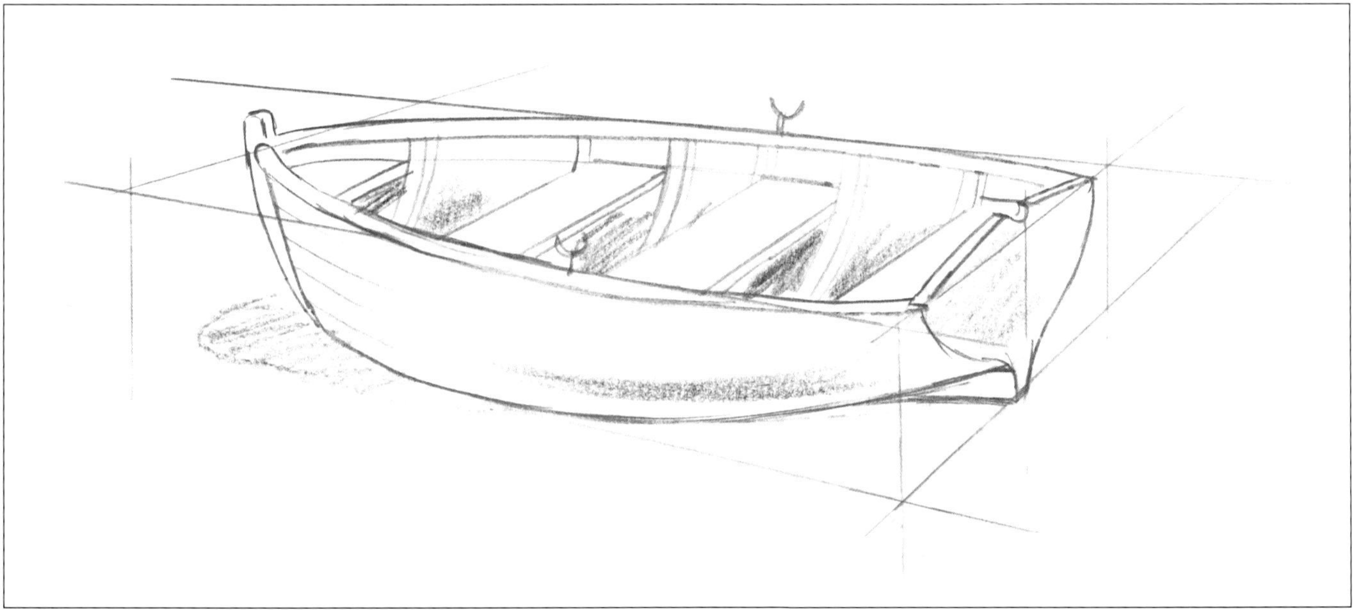

PROJECT ONE: Basic Landscape

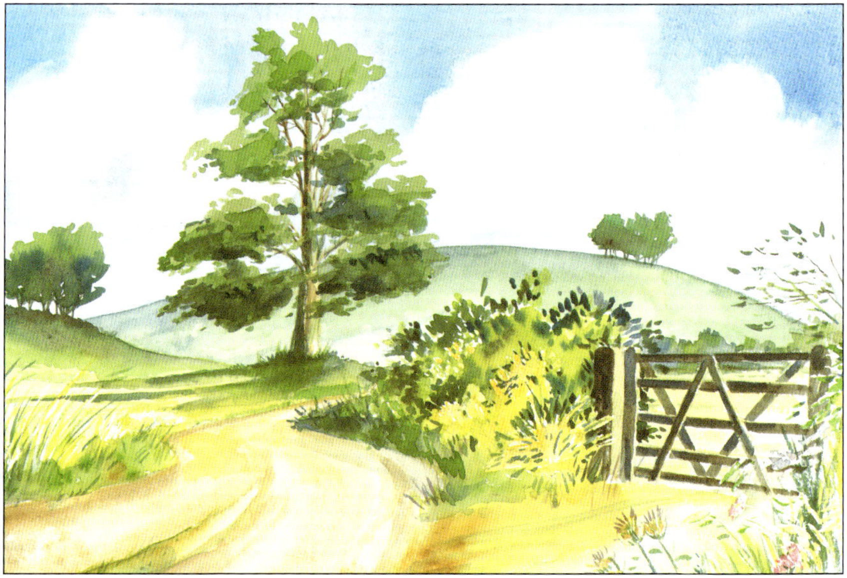

When painting landscape scenes, there is no need to pick a complex subject. A relatively sparse landscape can be more attractive than one with many focal points fighting for attention.

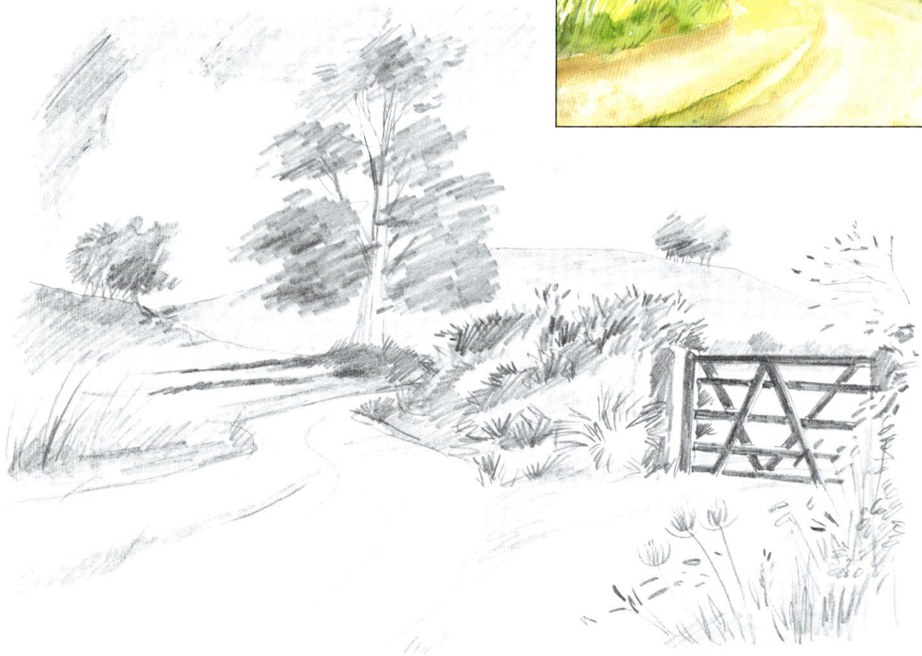

1. Sketch or trace the line drawing on page 90. Use the sketch above to establish tonal values. Pencil in the main shapes, making sure you are aware of where the light is coming from and where the highlights will fall on your subject.

Basic Landscape

2. Wash in the sky areas with different shades of blue. When painting sky, start with the darkest blue, so that the colour gradually fades to a lighter blue. While the wash for the sky is still wet, you should dab out the colour with a damp tissue or sponge for the clouds.

Use a damp tissue or paper towel to dab out the colour for the clouds.

3. Next, add the background, gradually working forward to the near foreground areas. Rather than diluting, gradually add more and more of the new colour. Allow the colours to merge, but allow one area to dry before moving to a new one, to avoid unwanted bleeding.

For the background, grade from one colour to another, adding colour to the edge to give shape while the wash is still damp.

4. Use a pale wash to draw the track. Add colour to shape the edges, and dab off the colour in the middle of the track with a paper towel. Avoid filling the track with colour as it is better to give the impression of a lighter touch.

Use a pale yellow to light brown wash to draw the track.

5. To create the green-blue effect in the background trees and shrubs, use the wet-in-wet technique. While the green foliage is still wet paint in the blue shading. The addition of this detail will help bring life to the foliage and to the painting as a whole.

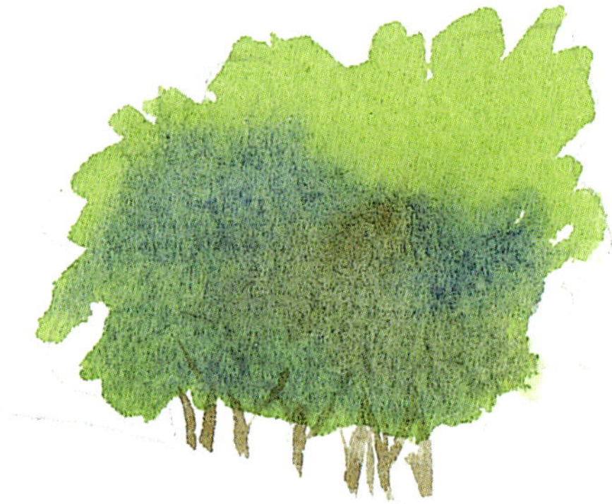

Add colour to the wash wet-in-wet to create this effect.

6. For the tree in the centre of the picture start with a green wash before adding more colour. When this is nearly dry, add the three darker colours. These will help to give shape and definition to the tree, one of the main focal points of the painting.

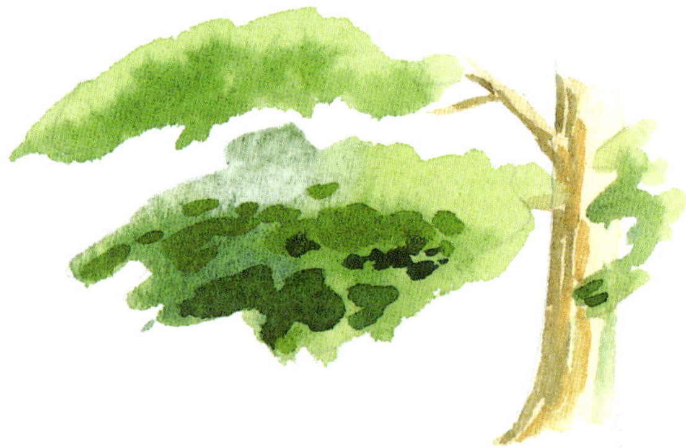

Adding detail to foliage will help to give your work definition.

7. Where you wish to keep areas of the painting white, use masking fluid (available from art shops) for the task. Follow the manufacturer's instructions and once the fluid is dry, add a wash of the appropriate colour. When the light colour is dry, add a darker colour. When this final colour is dry, remove the masking agent and paint over with the lightest colour if desired.

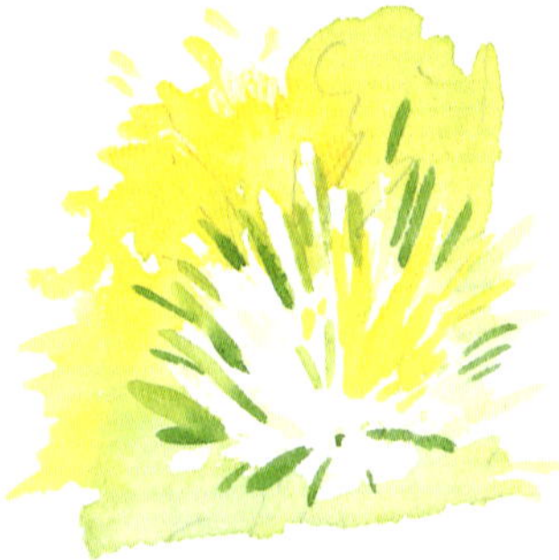

Use masking fluid to keep areas white. If necessary, this can be painted over later.

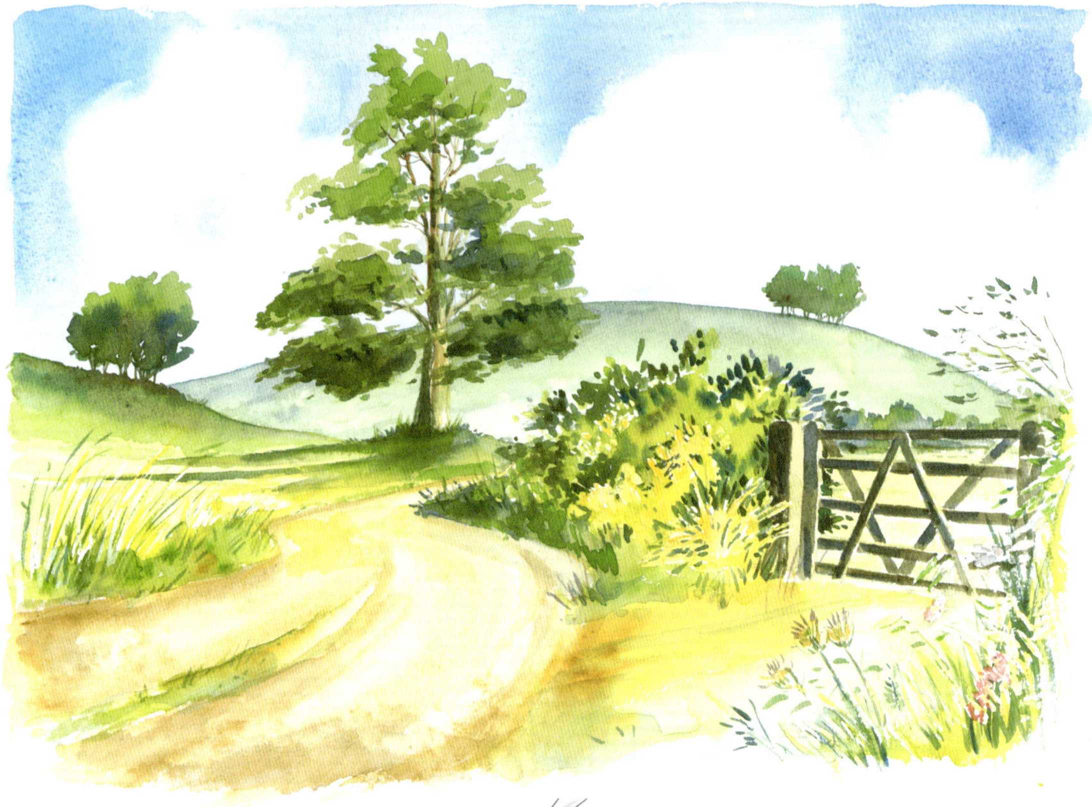

PROJECT TWO: Detailed Landscape

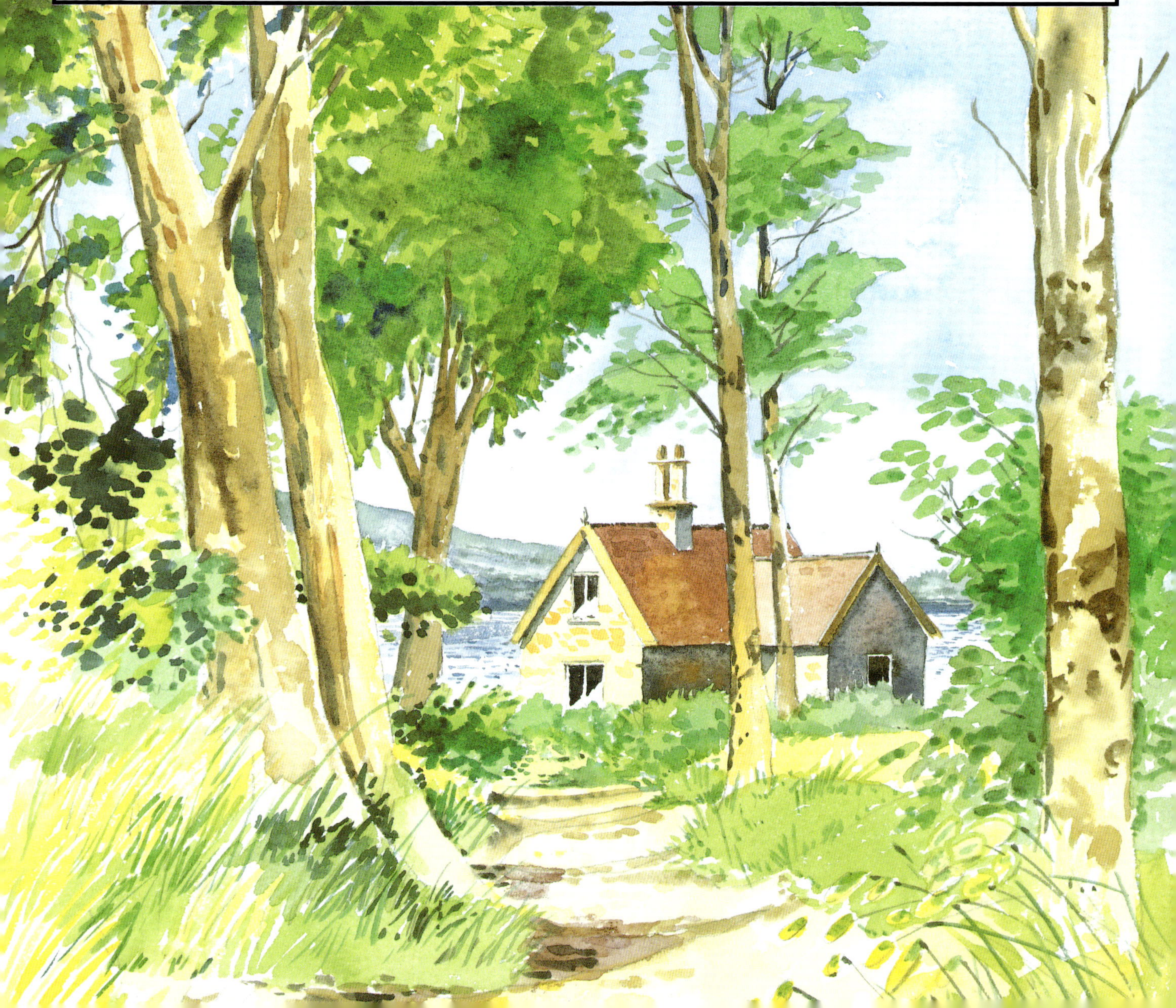

Detailed Landscape

Painting a more detailed landscape offers a different challenge to a simple one, but can turn out to be more rewarding.

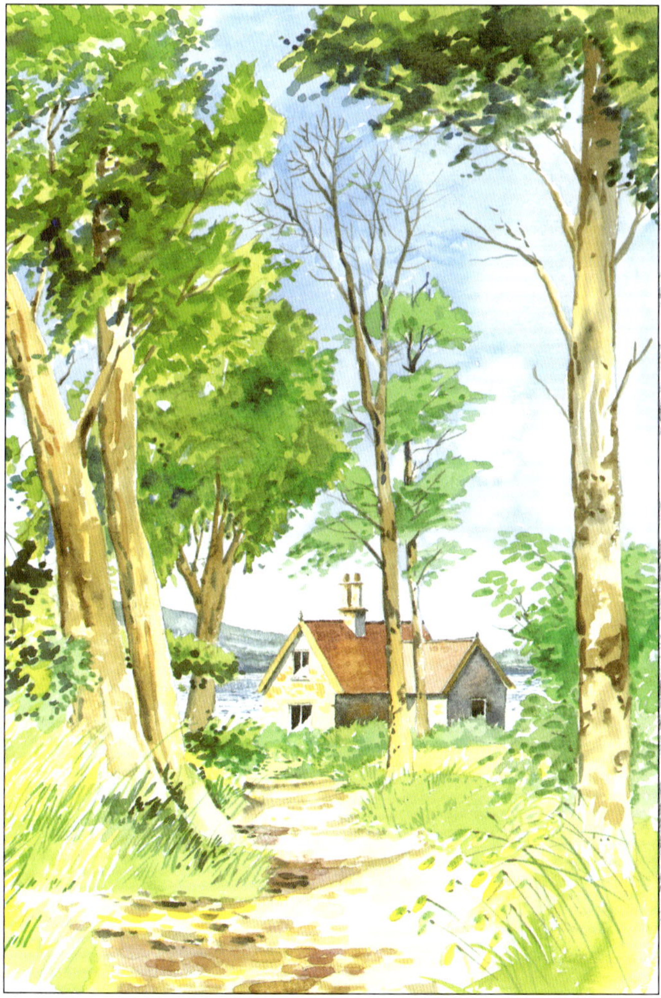

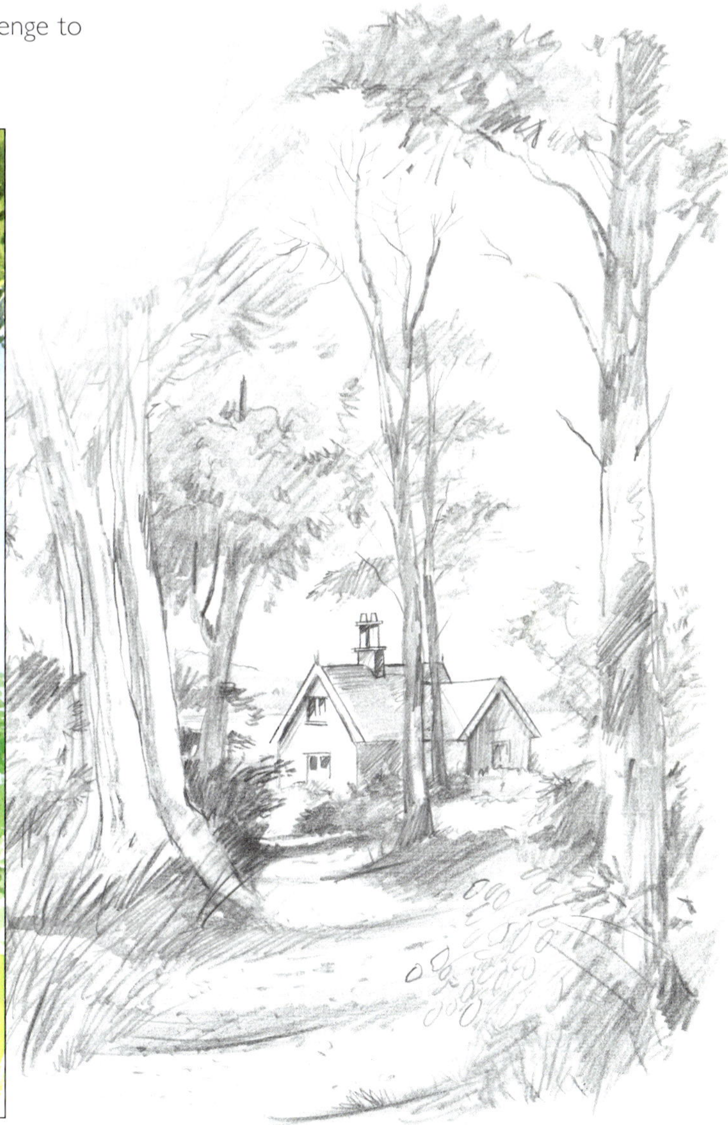

Detailed Landscape

1. Begin by sketching or tracing the line drawing on page 91. The sketch on page 31 can be used to establish tonal values. Pencil in the main shapes, always considering where the light is coming from and where the highlights are to fall on your subject.

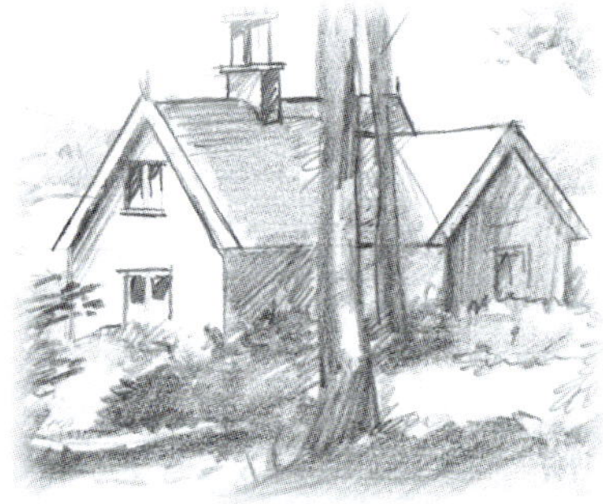

2. Wash in the sky areas with different shades of blue, leaving the areas of foliage white. If you like, use a liquid mask to keep the relevant areas white. When painting sky, start with the darkest blue before adding water to the pigment, so that the colour gradually fades to a lighter blue. When this is dry, add a pale green wash for the tree foliage.

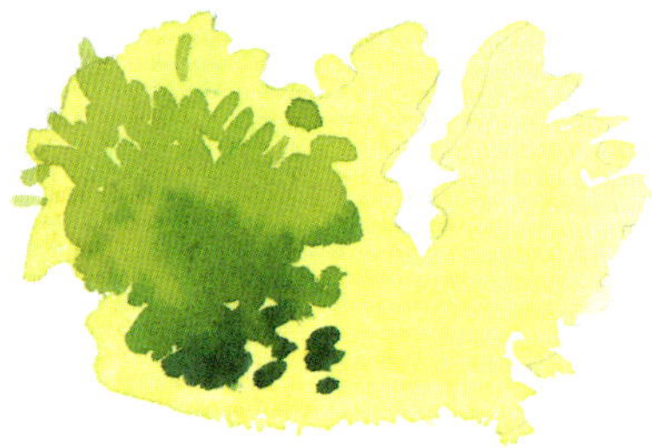

When the pale green wash is dry, add more colour to shape the foliage, adding dark colour wet-in-wet.

3. For the grass, use the lightest colour first, adding progressively darker colours. Let each colour dry before adding the new one. Apply a wash to the tree trunk first. Let this dry, then add a light colour, gradually getting slightly darker. Let this dry, then add the darkest colour wet-in-wet in some areas for texture.

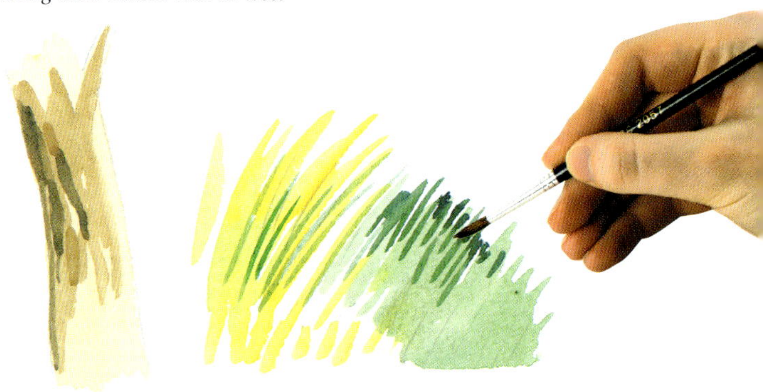

When the tree foliage is dry, work on the ground details. Put down the lightest colours in the foliage and foreground grass, path and tree trunks first.

Detailed Landscape

4. With the sky and greenery complete, you can start work on the house and distant hills. Each distinct area of the house should be painted on dry paper except for the roof, which should be painted wet-in-wet.

For the house, only the roof should be painted wet-in-wet.

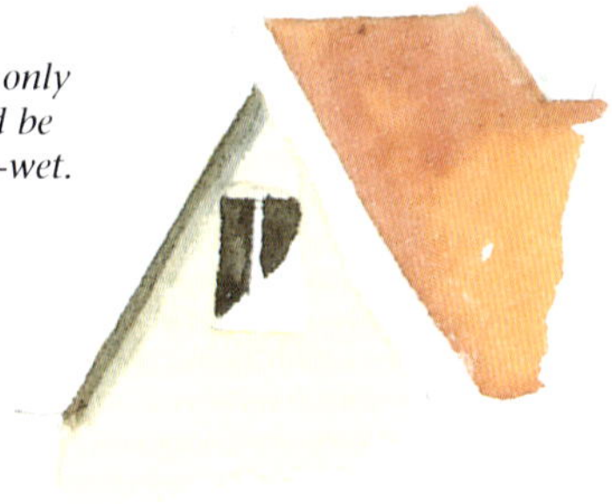

5. Continue using the wet-in-wet technique for the hills in the distance. In this instance, you will find it easier to scrape out white detail in the water with a knife rather than using a masking agent.

Use the wet-in-wet technique for the hills. For the water, scrape out white detail in the water with a knife rather than using a masking agent.

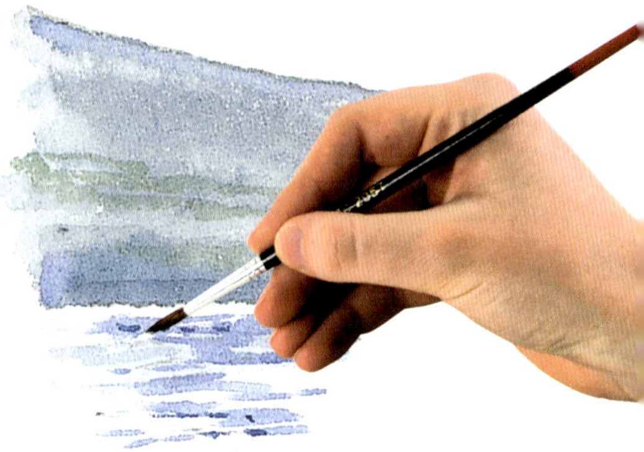

6. Complete the landscape by working on the path. Start by using successive washes, then begin to vary and build up the colour – this will help to make your picture look more three-dimensional.

Use successive washes for the path. Varying the colour will help to make your picture more three-dimensional.

PROJECT THREE: Harbour Scene

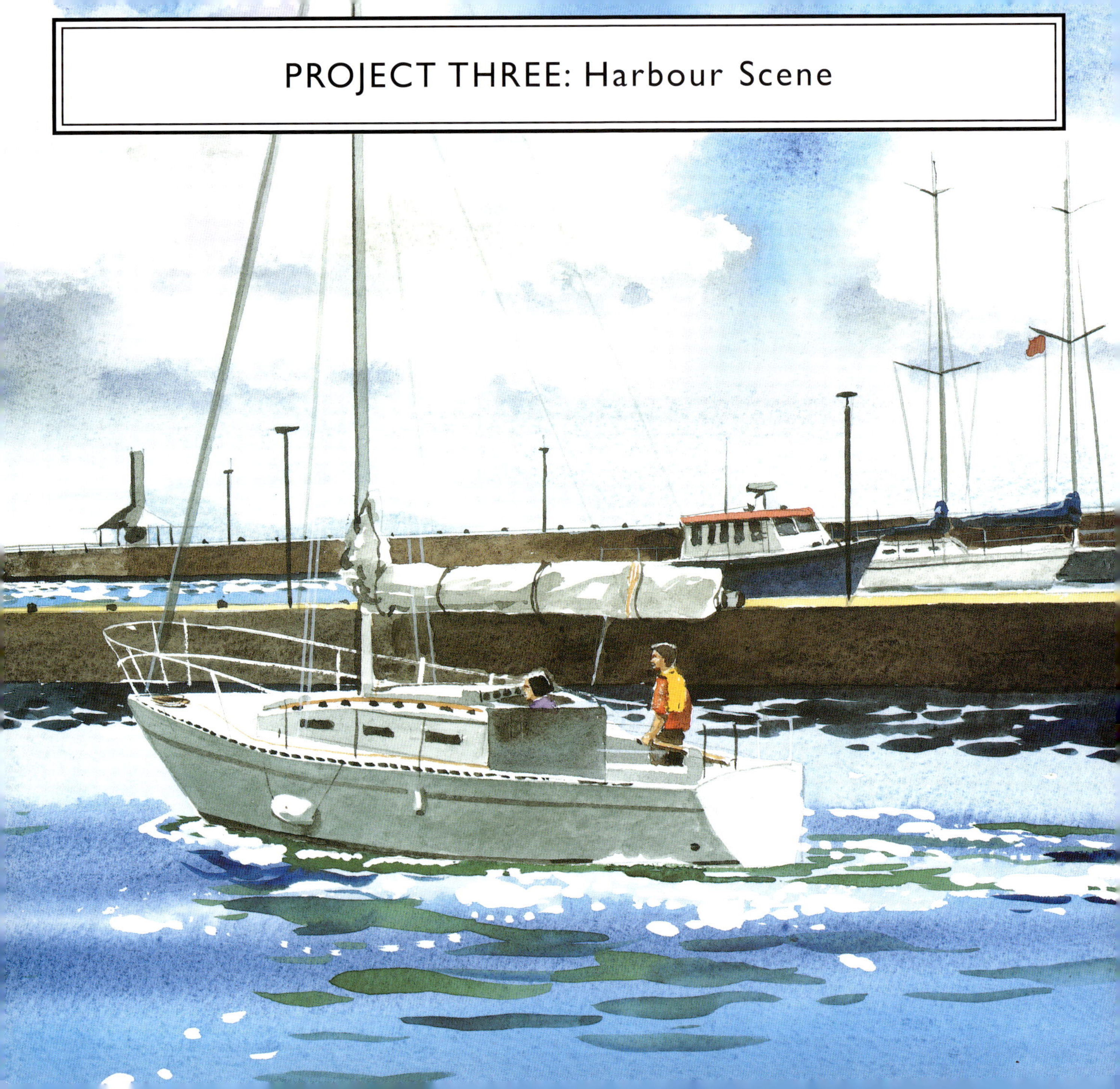

Harbour Scene

1. Sketch or trace the line drawing on page 95. Use the close-up sketch here to establish tonal values. Pencil in the main shapes, thinking about where the light is coming from and where the highlights will be in the painting.

First, lightly sketch the main shapes using drawing pencils.

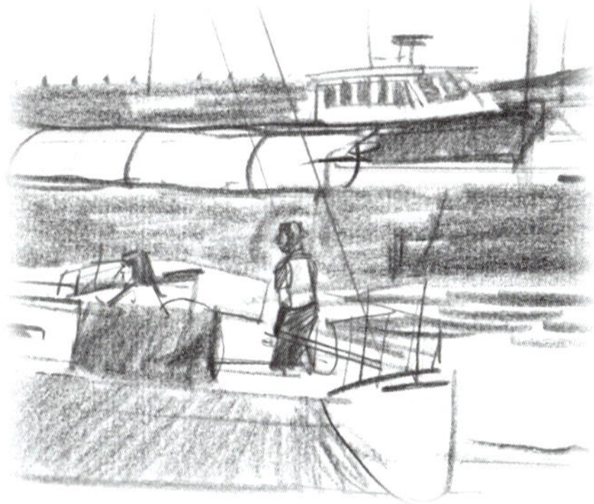

2. Wash in the sky areas with different shades of blue. Start with the darkest blue, before adding water to the pigment, so that the colour gradually fades to a lighter blue. As the cloud cover is more substantial in this project, you should paint them using the wet-in-wet technique.

The cloud is established using the wet-in-wet technique.

3. As with the sky, add a graduated wash for the sea. Use different shades of blue, starting with the darkest, then add water to the pigment to create lighter shades. When the wash is dry, add a brownish wash for the harbour walls before adding the detail to it.

Add the wash for the harbour wall area before adding the detail.

Harbour Scene

4. As with the harbour wall, add a simple wash for the foreground boat. The details can be added when this is dry. Also, paint the shadows of the sea, covering the highlighted areas with masking fluid. The white areas around the boat will help to give it a sense of movement.

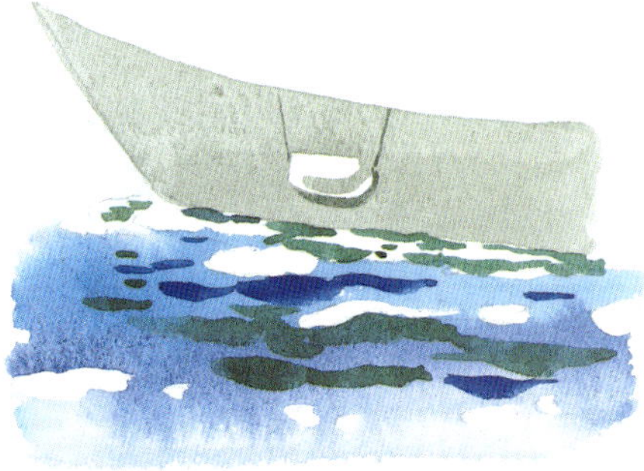

Paint the shadows of the sea, covering the highlighted areas with masking fluid.

5. It is not necessary to go into a great deal of detail for the figures on the boat so use simple colours. Having said that, take care with skin tones or you run the risk of ruining the quality of the picture over a small point of interest.

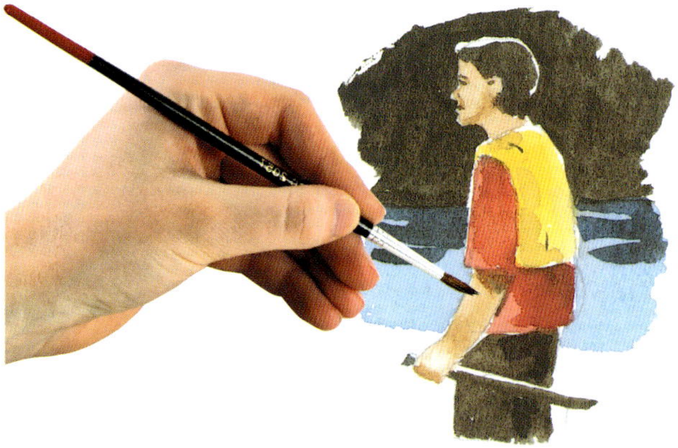

Use simple colours for the figure.

6. For the detail of the boats in the background, you should begin by adding the lighter colours first. Complete with the darker colours of the boats' windows and hulls when these are dry.

For the detail in all the boats, add the lighter colours before completing with the darker ones.

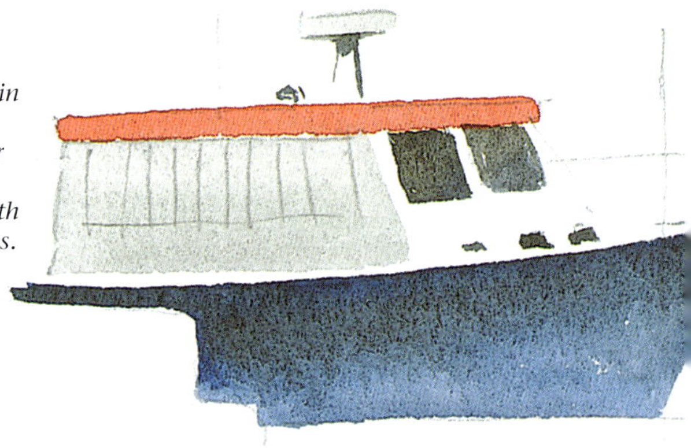

Harbour Scene

7. Add the details to the boat in the foreground last. Use a rigger brush for the lines of the boat as these are ideal for adding fine details. However, if you don't feel confident with a rigger brush, use a ruler instead. With the edge lifted, carefully run the brush along it to get straight lines.

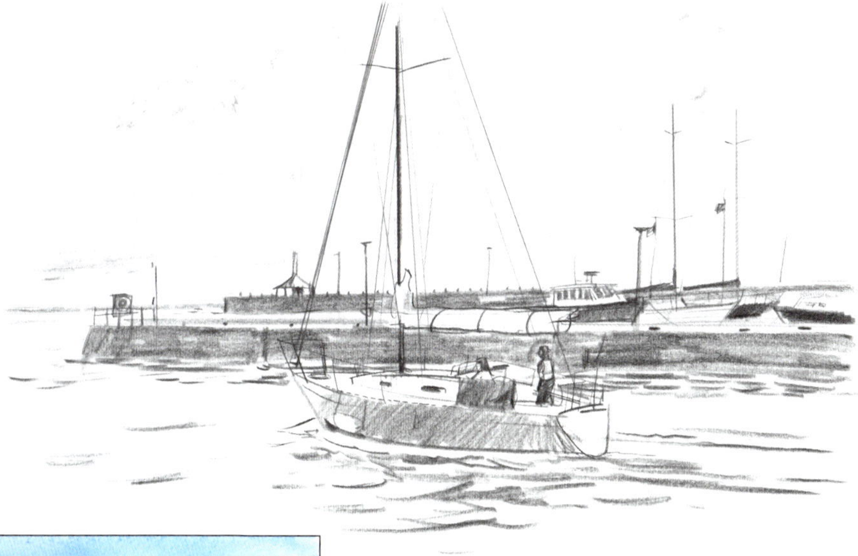

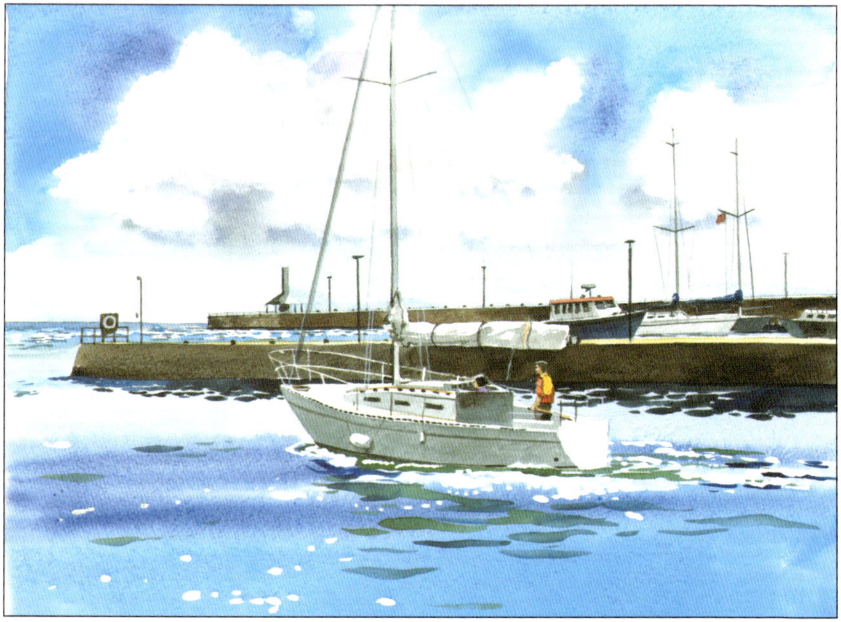

Painting harbour scenes requires a greater knowledge of drawing. No one is going to notice a misplaced branch on a tree, but a boat mast must be painted at the right angle.

PROJECT FOUR: Basic Still Life

Here is a simple, but well-composed selection of beautiful pears. These pears have a fantastic range of colours, which are contrasted against the deep blue tablecloth.

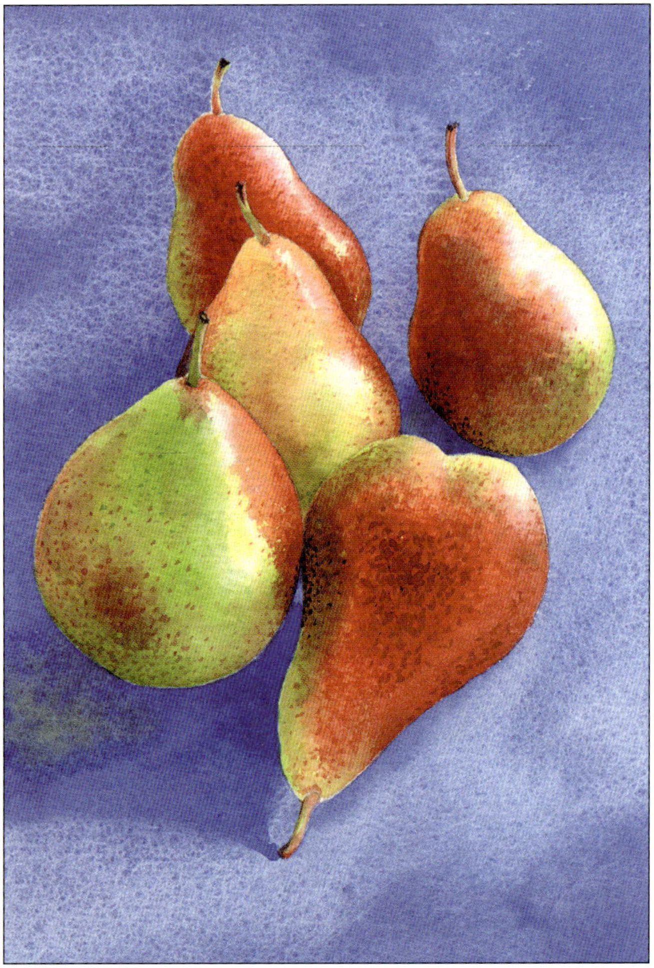

1. Lightly draw an outline of your composition, being careful not to mark or dent the paper too much (you can rub out any pencil lines when your painting is dry and complete).

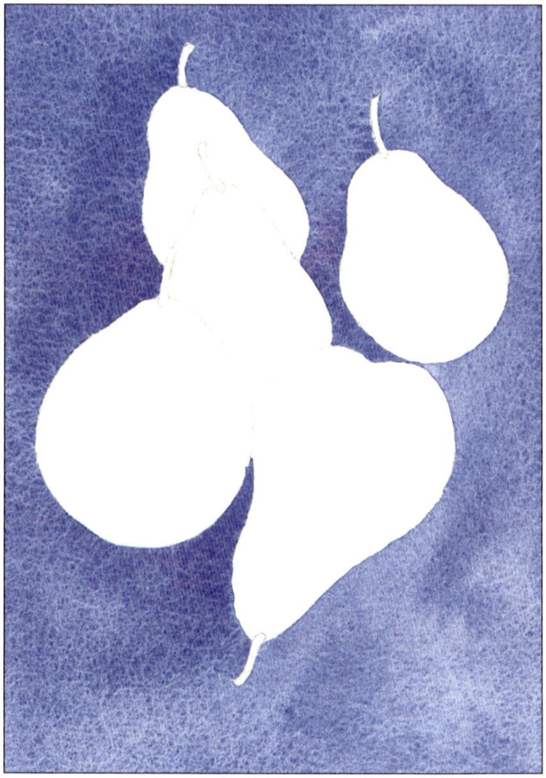

2. Make up an ultramarine wash and add in a small amount of diluted alizarin crimson. Wet the background area and then add in the ultramarine with a few dabs of alizarin crimson to give a bit of variation.

3. Mix up some lemon yellow for the pears. Wet the paper and drop in the paint, leaving the paper white where the highlights are (in this composition the light source is coming in from the top right so all the highlights will occur roughly in these positions on the pears). If the highlights fill with yellow then lift them out with a clean, semi-wet paintbrush, or dab them out with a piece of tissue.

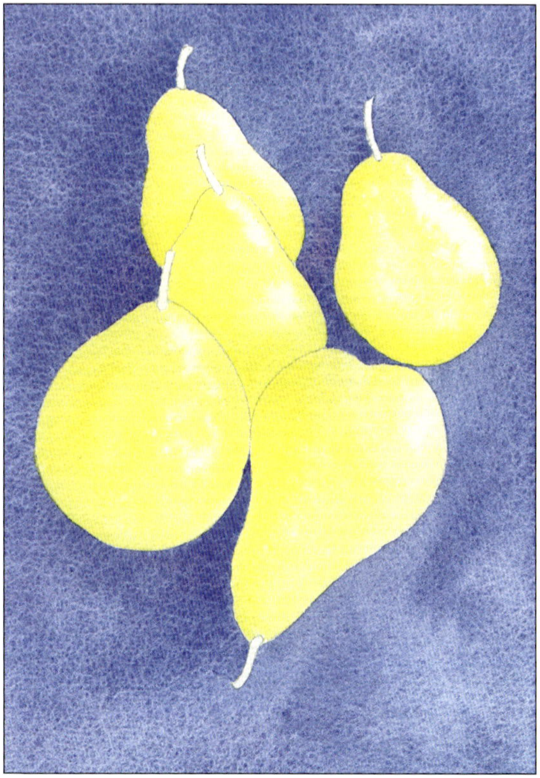

4. For the green tones, mix up sap green, lemon yellow and yellow ochre. Wet the pears again, then drop the green into the appropriate places. These will be the natural colour variations within the fruit but also in the more shaded areas.

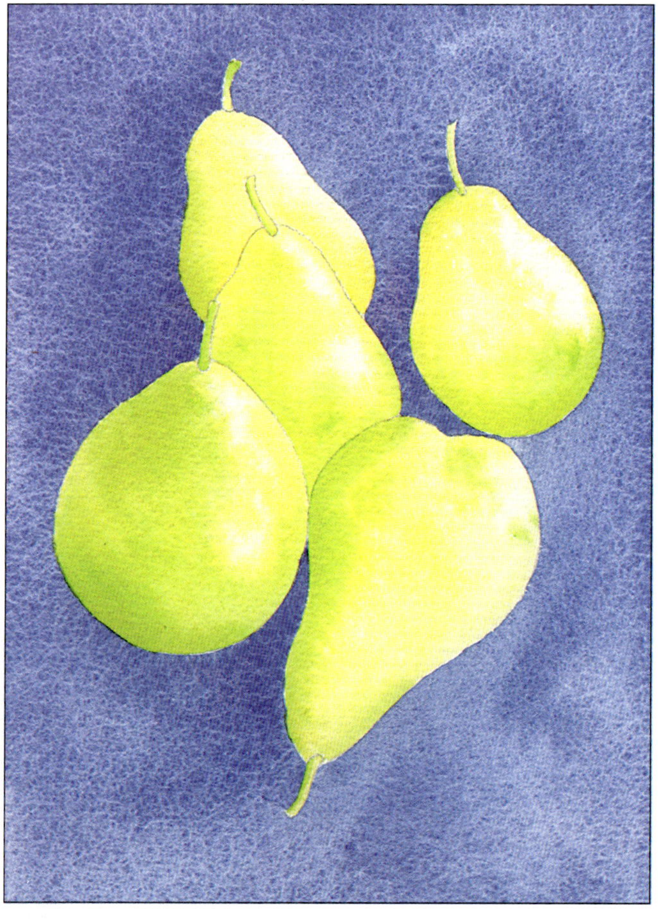

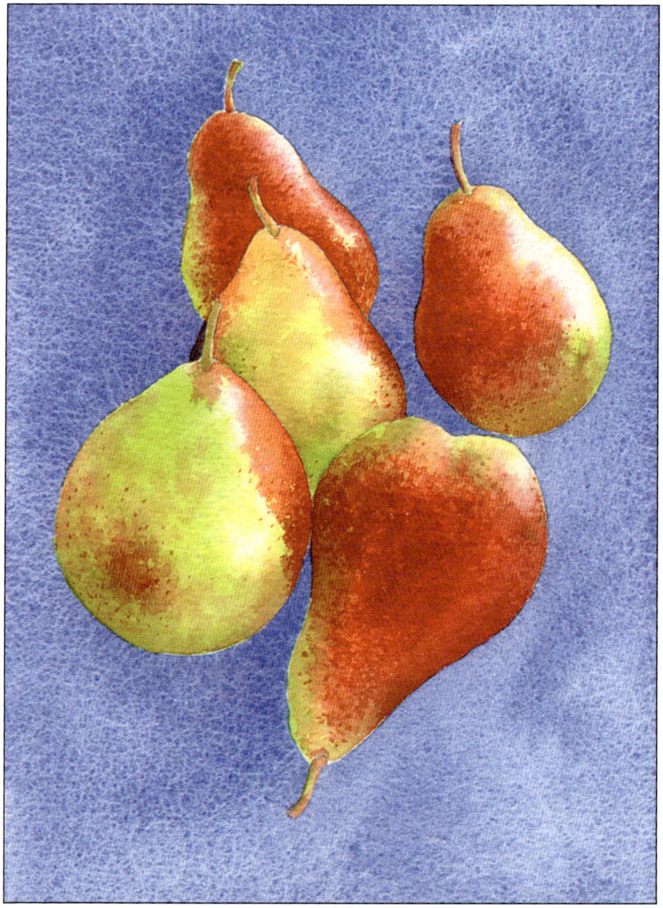

5. Then, mix alizarin crimson with lemon yellow for the reds. Wet the pears again and drop in the colour. Some of the red areas should be quite blotchy, so gently touch the tip of the brush onto the paper to achieve this effect.

6. To create the cloth shadows, make up two strong mixes, one of ultramarine and one of ultramarine with alizarin crimson. Also, mix up a sap green with lemon yellow. You don't need to wet the paper first, just paint in the shaded areas, soften the edges, then drop in some of the yellow-green mix for the reflected colour of the pears. Remember to note the shape of the shadows, in particular, the way the stalk of the foremost pear has a smaller shadow as it touches the cloth.

7. Paint the deepest shadows on the pears. To do this, mix up a very pale wash of sap green and alizarin crimson and apply to the shaded areas. When dry, add in the more detailed speckles of the pears, with the appropriate colours.

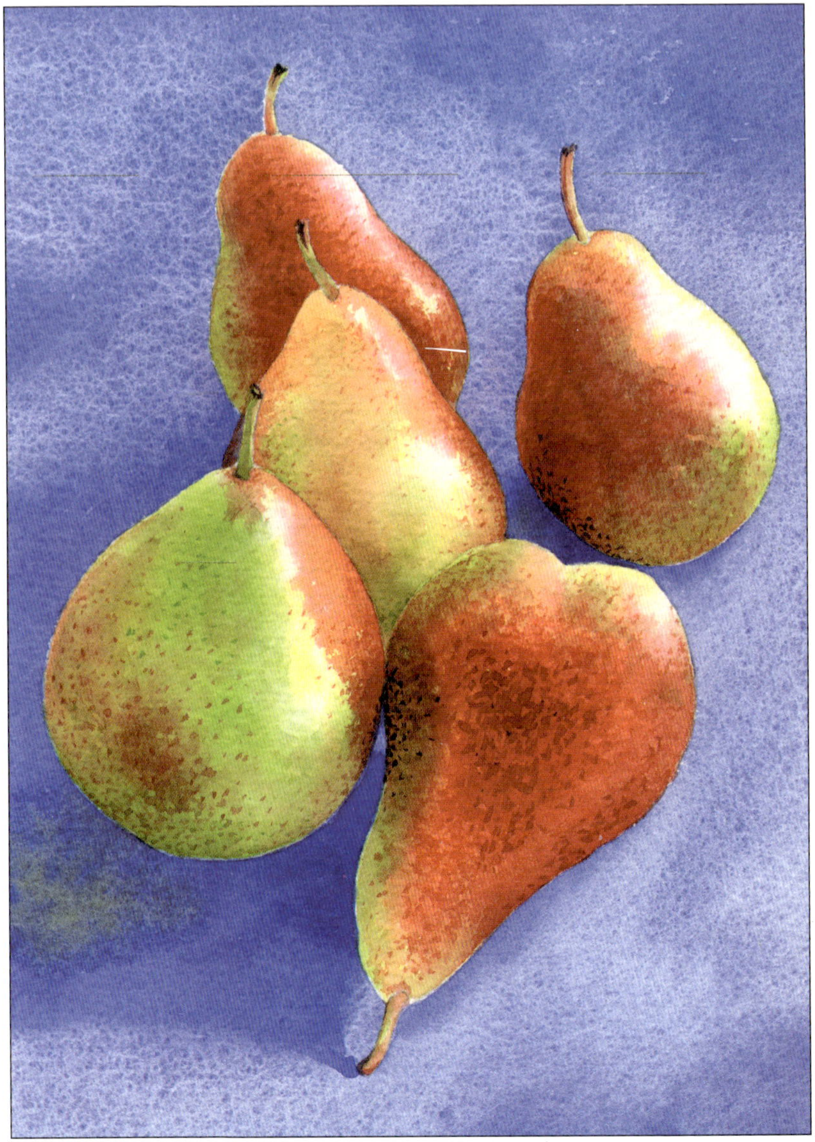

PROJECT FIVE: Still Life Study Two

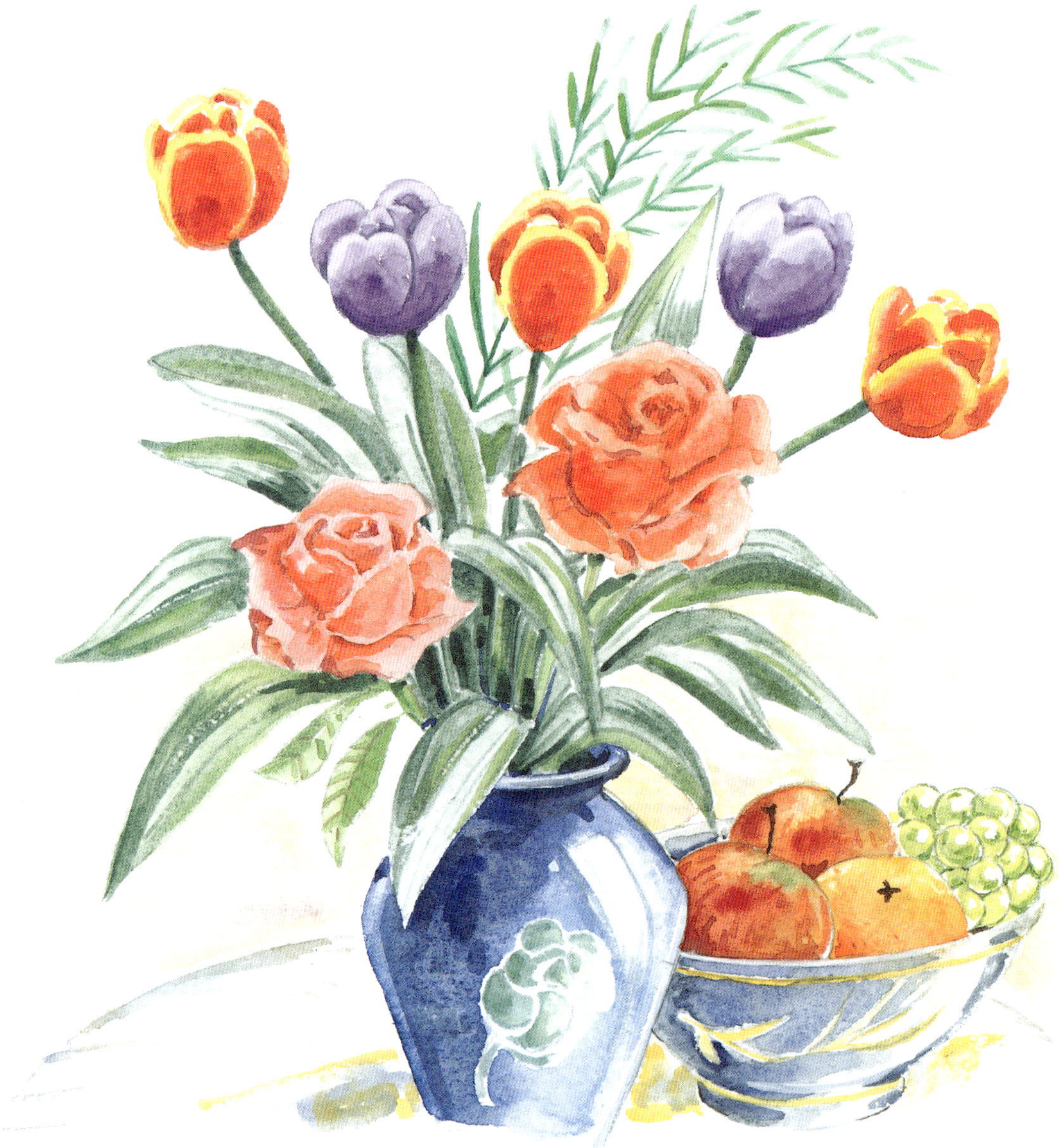

Still Life Study Two

The advantage of painting still life is the degree of control it offers. You can control the lighting, the size, the shape and the colour of your object.

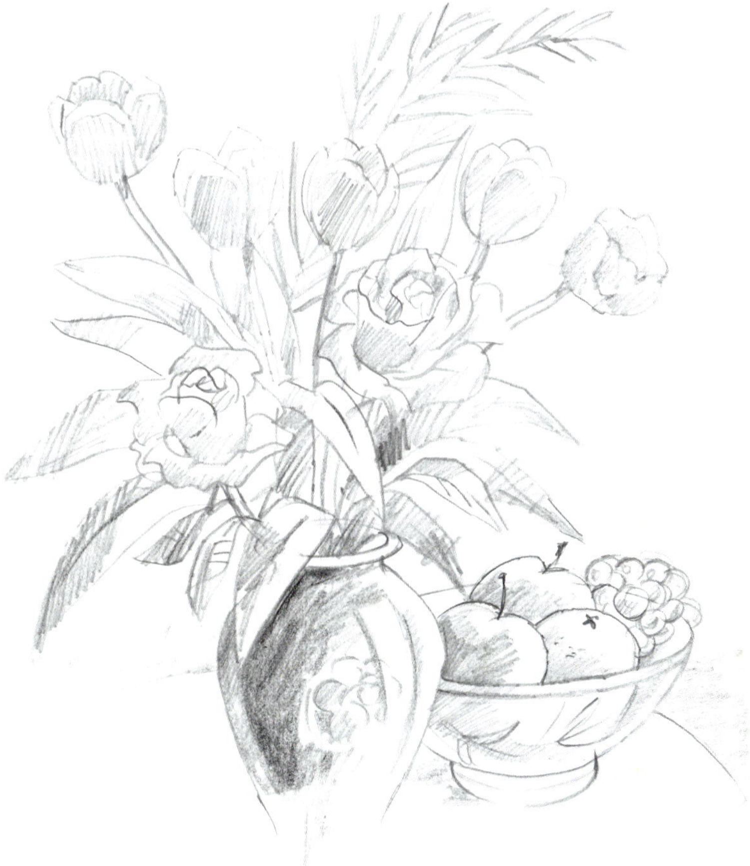

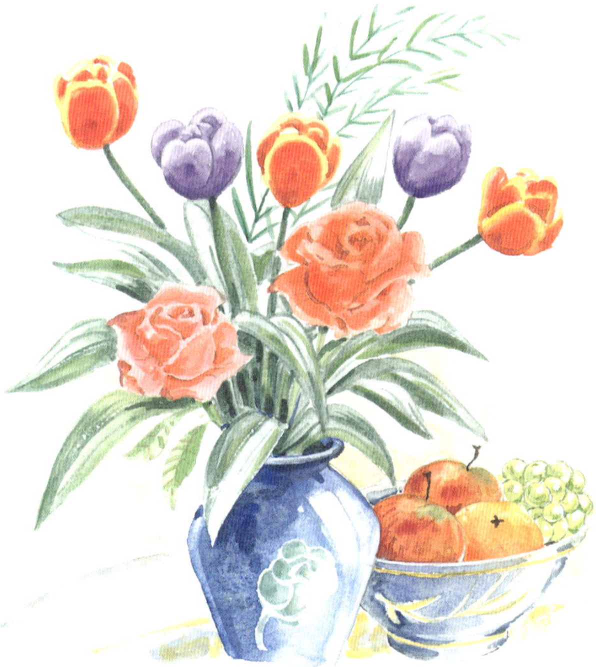

Still Life Study Two

1. Sketch or trace the line drawing on page 92. Use the close-up sketch here to establish tonal values. Use a pencil for the main shapes, making sure you are aware of where the light is coming from and where the highlights will fall on your subject.

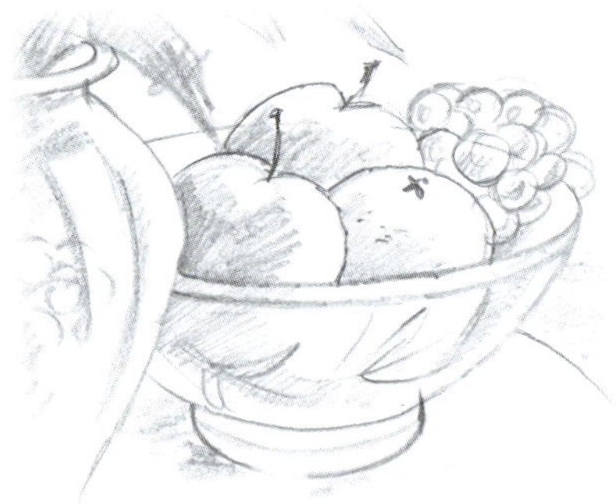

2. Flowers are created with a wash of the lightest colour. While this is wet, remove sections of paint for the lightest areas with a dry, clean brush. Use wet-in-wet to add darker colours, moulding the shape of the petals. When almost dry, add the detail of the darkest areas. For the tulips work on the yellow areas first. When this is nearly dry, add a pale version of the red so that the yellow and red blend together. Then, add darker reds to mould the shape of the petals.

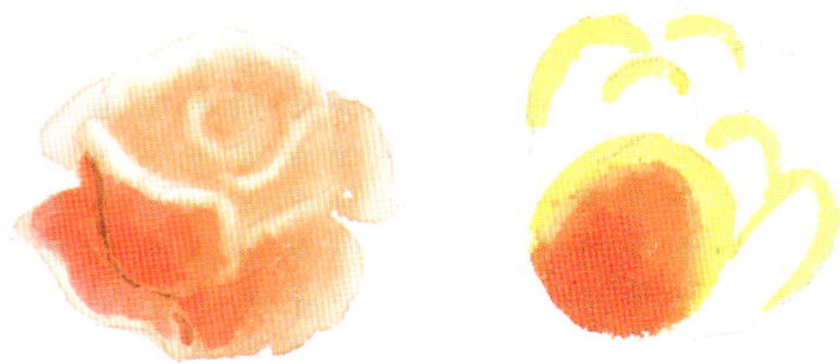

Use a wash of the lightest colour for the flowers. The wet-in-wet technique should be used to add darker colours, moulding the shape of the petals.

3. For the leaves, use a pale wash first. Lift off the colour for the lightest-coloured areas with a damp paper towel. When this is almost dry, add the darker colour to shape the leaf.

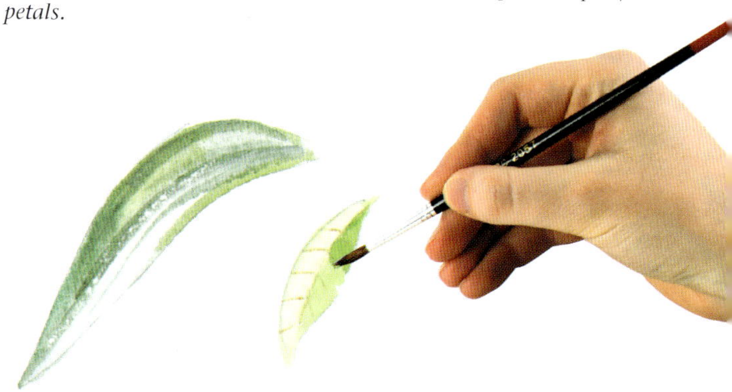

When all the washes for the leaves are dry, scrape off some of the colour with a sharp blade to reveal the textured highlights.

Still Life Study Two

4. In order to paint the vase and bowl, you should use the wet-in-wet technique. Start with a light wash, then remove some of the colour with a damp paper towel. Then, add the darker washes wet-in-wet, gradually building up the shape of the vase. When this is dry, finish off the detail of the darker areas.

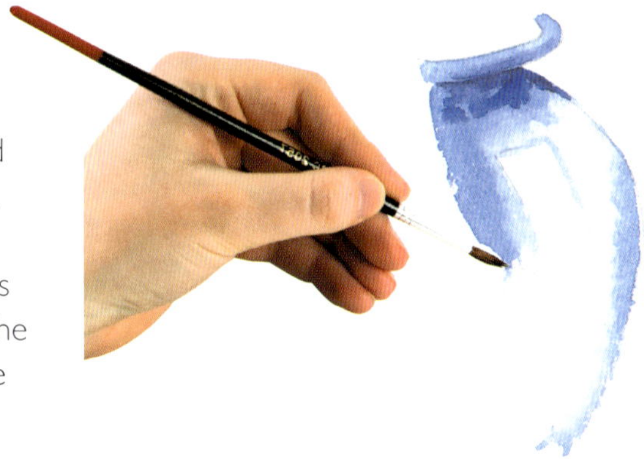

Use the wet-in-wet technique for the vase and bowl. Start with a light wash, adding darker washes to build up the shape.

5. You should also use the wet-in-wet technique to shape the various colours of the larger fruit. Once again, begin with a light wash before adding the darker colours for the shadows. When dry, add the final details.

The wet-in-wet technique is also used to shape the colours of the larger fruit.

6. For the grapes, use a pale wash. Use a masking agent to reserve the white highlight. As always, it is this attention to detail that will improve the quality of your work. Add the slightly darker colour wet-in-wet and the final details when this is dry.

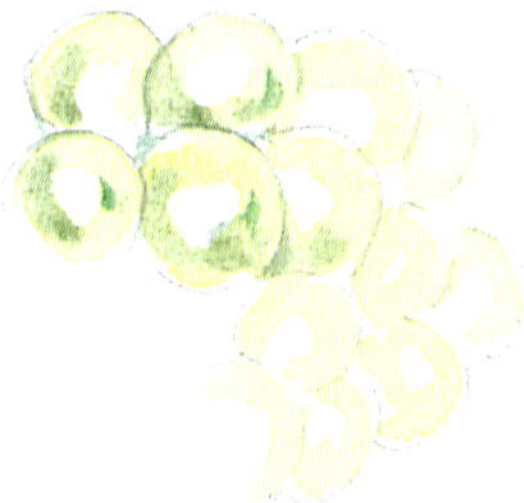

Use a masking agent for the white highlights of the grapes and a pale green wash for the remainder.

PROJECT SIX: Detailed Still Life

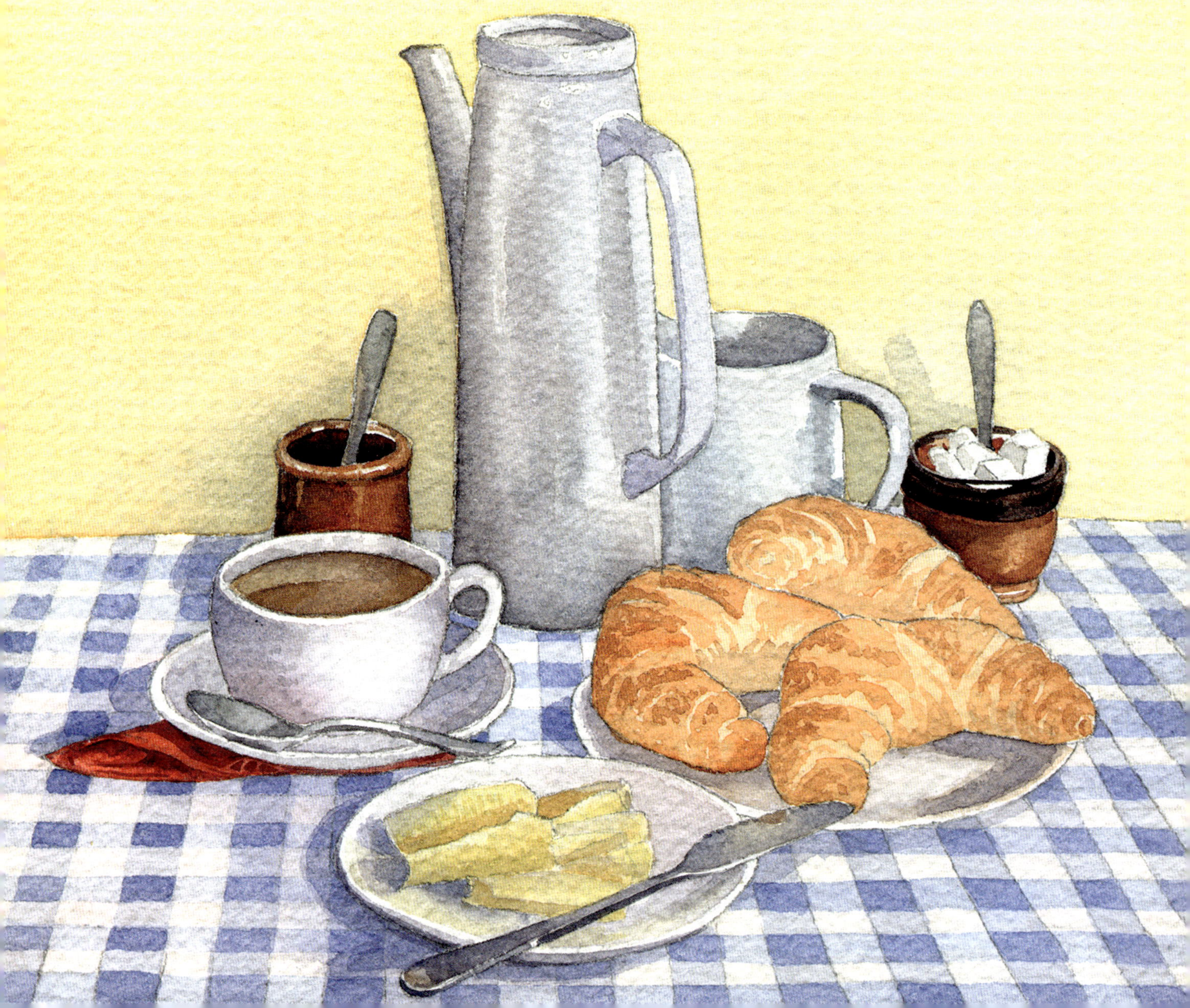

Detailed Still Life

Still life pictures are a good way to improve your painting skills, as your subject matter will remain constant, enabling you to take your time.

1. Using an HB pencil, draw out your still life, adding as much detail as necessary. You will need to pay a lot of attention to the checked tablecloth as there is a lot of perspective involved.

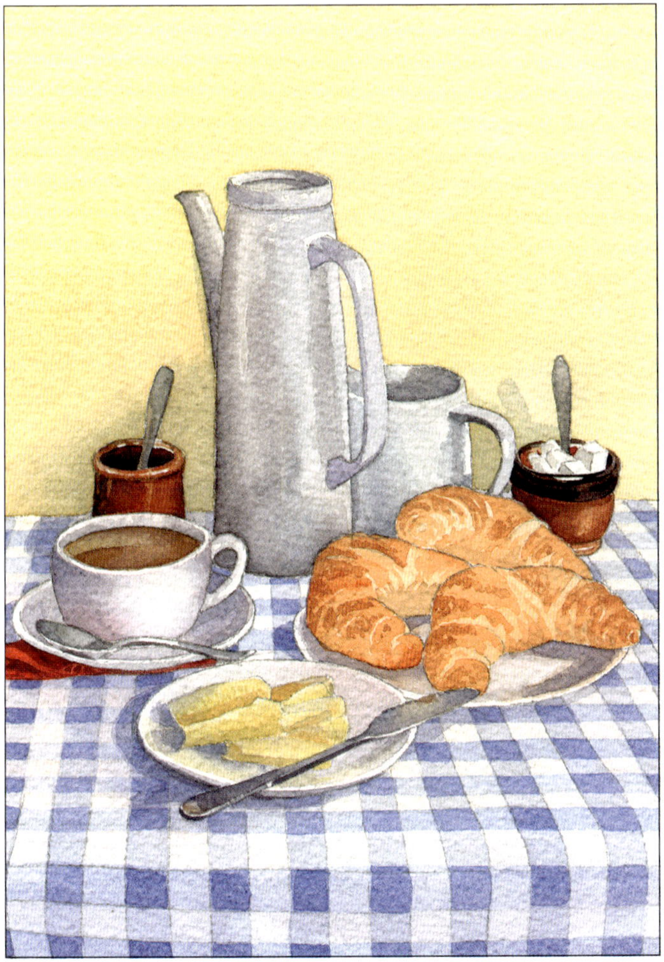

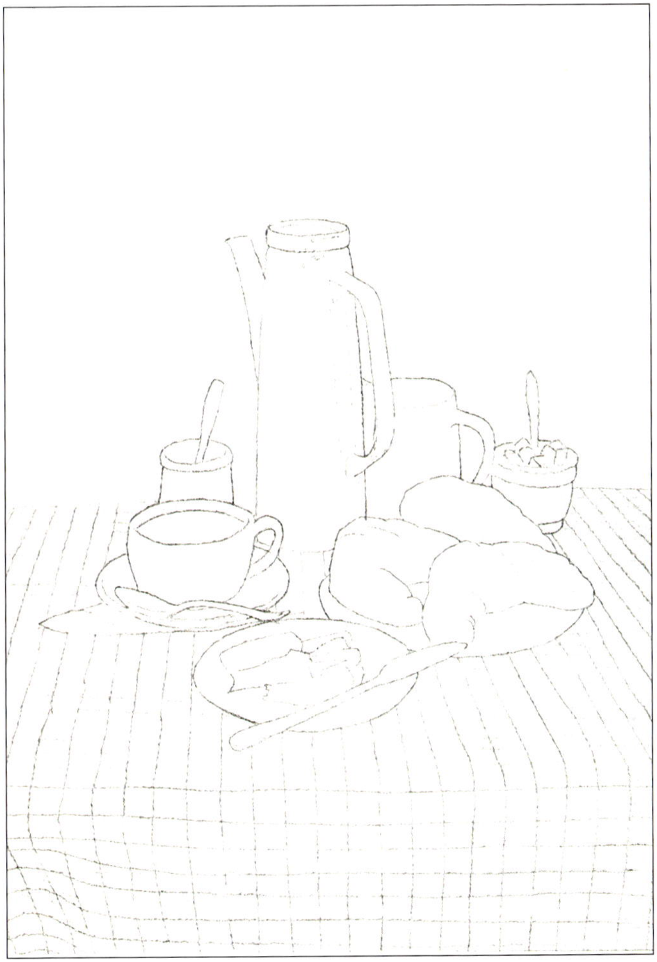

Detailed Still Life

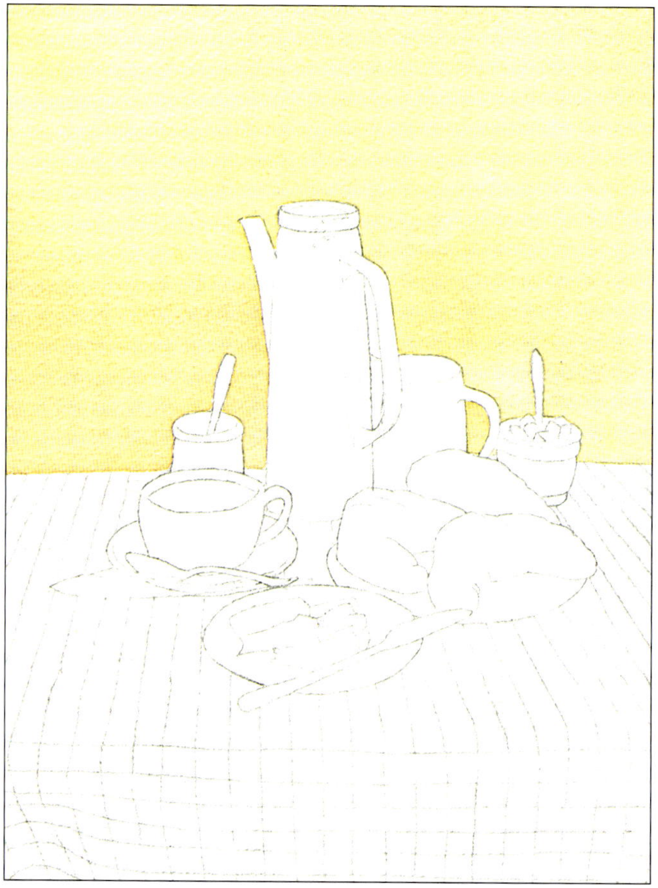

2. Paint in a simple background using a wash of yellow ochre. Then, introduce a small amount of burnt sienna into the bottom left of the background and then a little ultramarine at the top. This background colour will create a nice contrast with the blue of the tablecloth.

3. Mix up a dilute ultramarine and paint in all of the vertical blue lines in the tablecloth. At this stage, you should not attempt to create any differences in the tone of the blue lines. You will start to notice how effective your perspective is at this stage.

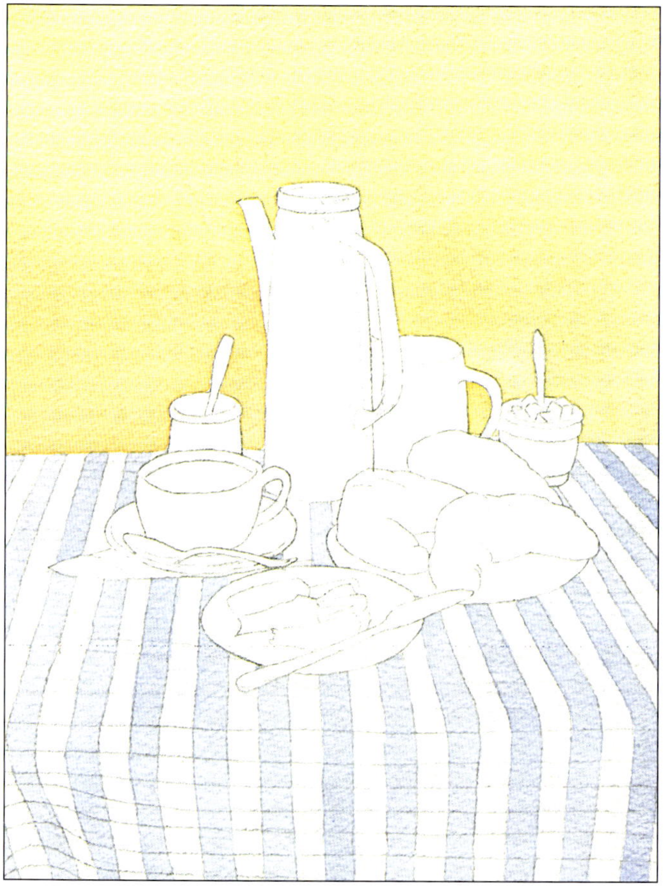

Detailed Still Life

4. With the same mixture of ultramarine, once the vertical blue lines are dry, add in the horizontal blue lines of the tablecloth. Again, perspective plays its part; these lines should be thicker when they are nearer to you and thinner when they are further away. You will notice that you have created a third blue where the vertical and horizontal lines overlap.

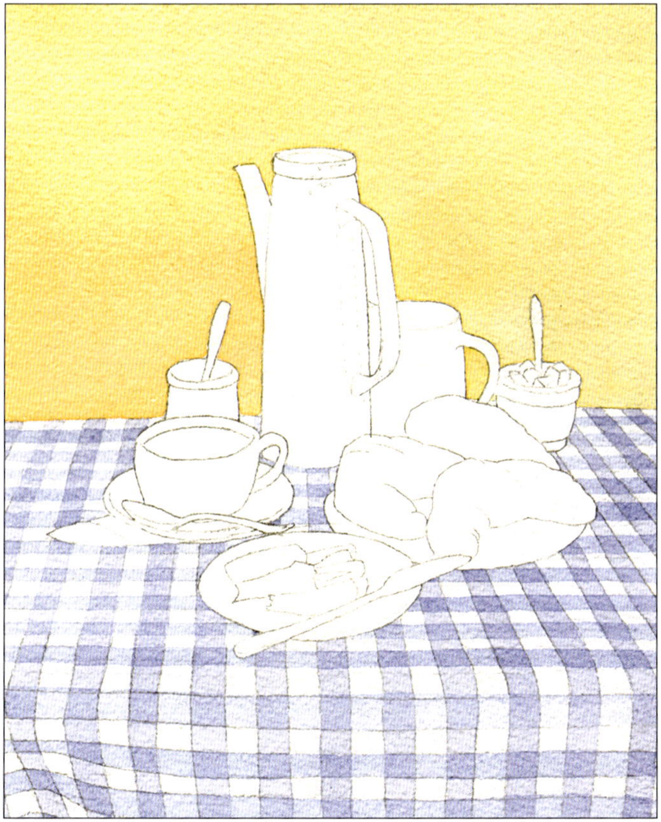

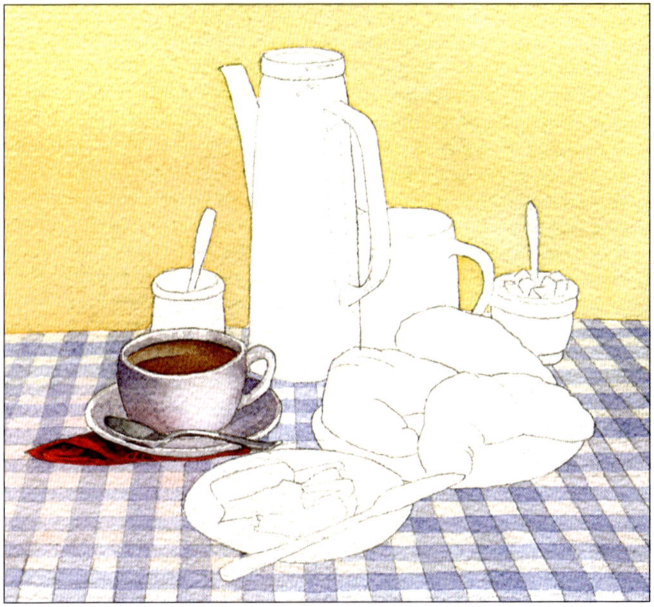

5. Paint the coffee cup with the red napkin underneath it. Begin with a medium mixture of yellow ochre, burnt sienna and ultramarine for the coffee. Leave the area where the cup is reflected and use a clean, wet brush to soften the top and right edges of the reflection; leave the bottom as a harder edge. Paint the napkin with alizarin crimson, darkening into the folds by adding ultramarine. Then, mix up differing amounts of ultramarine and sepia to make the steel, grey colours of the spoon. Finally, use ultramarine mixed with alizarin crimson for the white cup and saucer; you can drop in a little crimson where it reflects the napkin.

Detailed Still Life

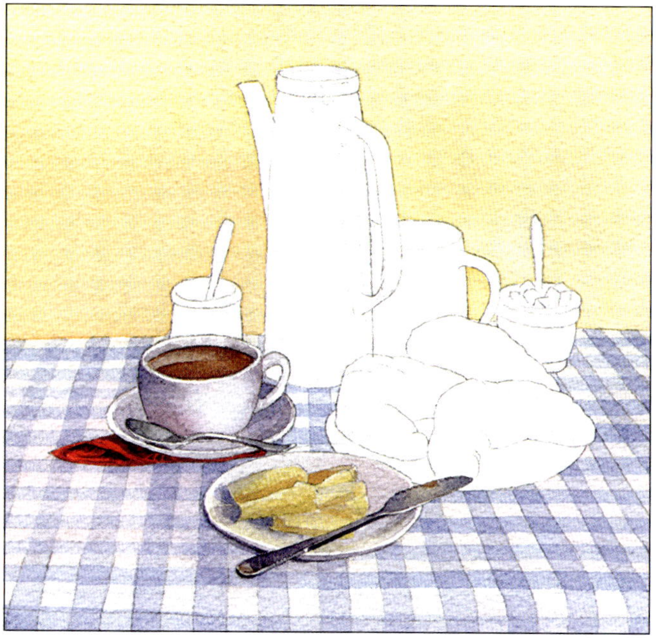

6. Next, paint the plate of butter, using the same colours for the knife as for the spoon, carefully observing the reflections of colour and highlights. Paint the plate in a similar way to the cup and saucer. Once it has dried, mix a delicate yellow from lemon yellow and yellow ochre; keep your colour pale and paint a flat wash over all the butter. Increase the intensity of the mixture where you need a little more colour and drop this stronger colour in while the paper is still slightly wet. Allow to dry, and then mix up a purple to use over the yellow where shadows are needed.

7. At the back of the painting you can now paint in the two earthen-coloured pots. Mix up the basic colours: a burnt sienna, alizarin crimson and sepia for the body colour; and a deep sepia and alizarin crimson mix for the rim of the sugar pot and for the inside of the jam pot. Make sure you leave any highlights on the rims. Paint the sugar cubes using the same tones as used for the tea cup and saucer.

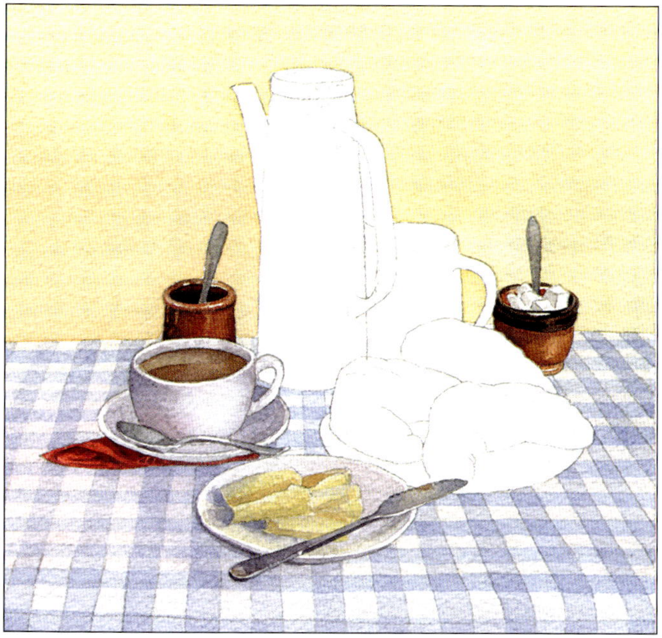

8. Paint the plate with the croissants on in the same way as the saucer and the butter plate. Mix up a wash of yellow ochre and burnt sienna and then paint a wash over the croissants. Let your paper dry slightly and over paint the same colour again to start indicating the folds in the pastry; add more burnt sienna into the mixture for the darker areas.

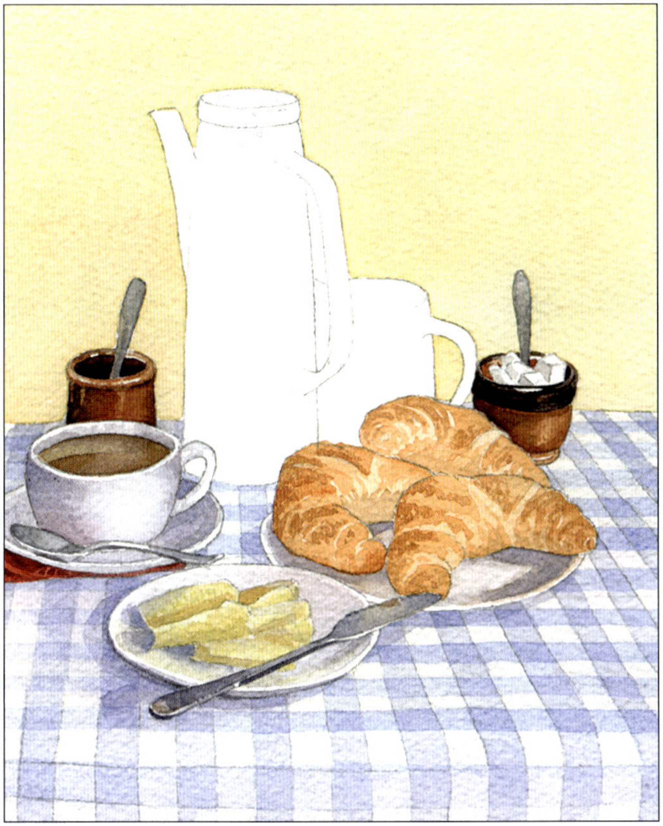

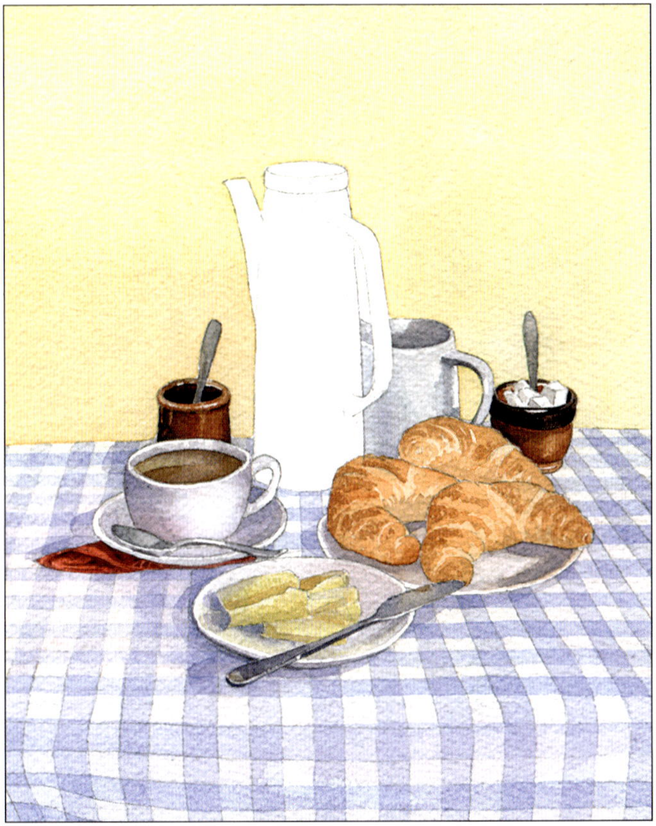

9. Now, paint the milk jug in a similar way as the rest of the crockery, with ultramarine mixed with alizarin crimson. You will also have to use a full range of tones from these colours for the handle.

10. For the coffee pot, use the same colours as for all of the crockery, but this time you have several features to define, such as the spout, handle and lid.

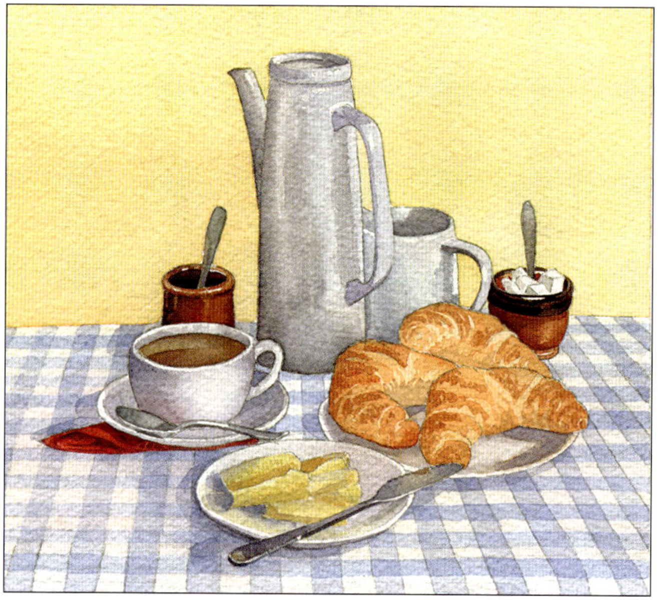

11. Complete your painting by adding in the shadows. Begin with the tablecloth at the back with a thin wash of ochre. Near the napkin use a thin wash of alizarin crimson. Mix a wash of crimson alizarin and ultramarine for the shadows underneath the plates and the front of the tablecloth. With a light blue-purple, add shadows from the pots onto the wall. Repaint the blue squares caused by the overlapping lines on the tablecloth with more ultramarine.

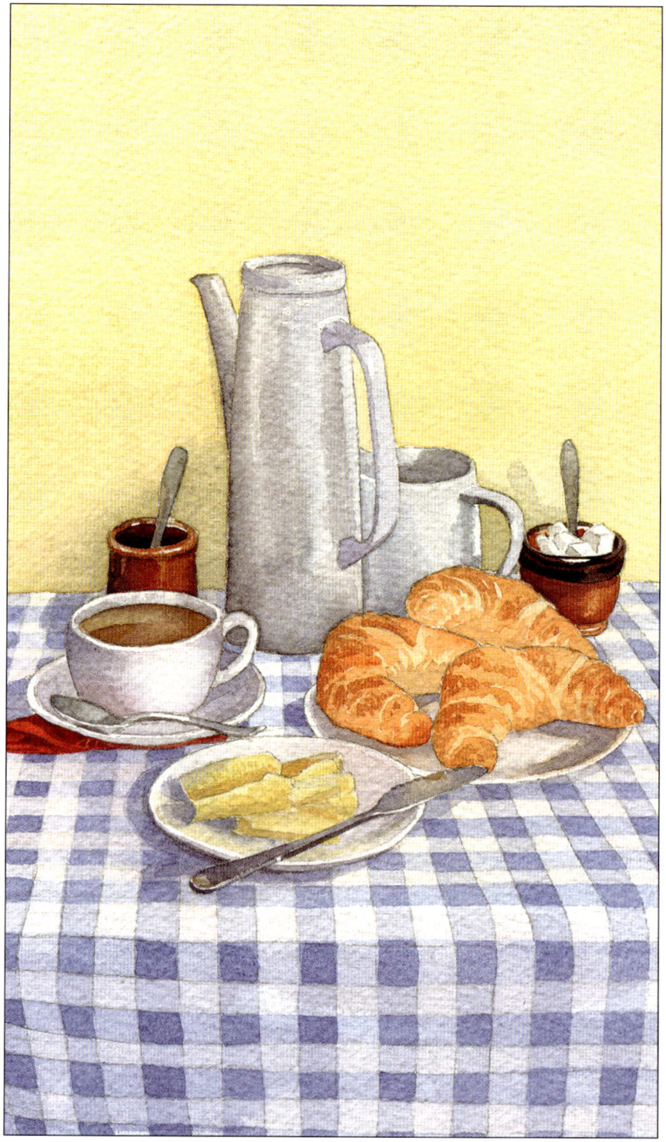

Drawing Animals

In the following pages there are some very simple ways to draw animals.

When drawing animals, look for the simple shapes. There are four animal drawing exercises featured here, which show the subjects broken down into simple shapes which are easier to draw.

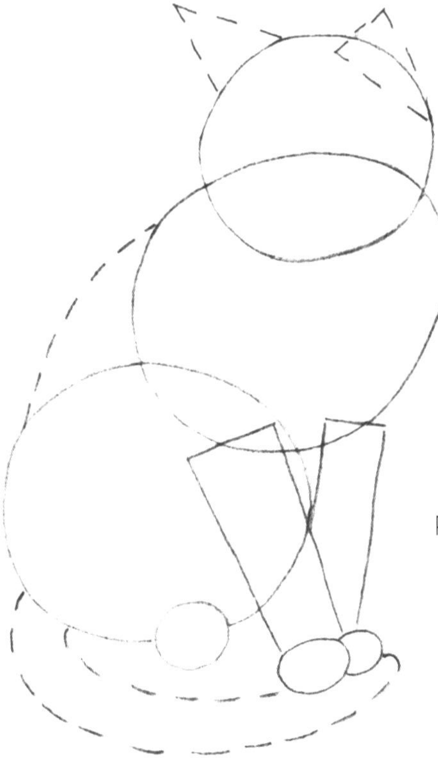

When you are drawing the shapes, use your pencil lightly (a B or 2B pencil is good for this) because you are just drawing a few guidelines, in a framework on which you will draw your finished picture.

Drawing a seated cat

Firstly, draw a circle for the cat's head, then join a larger egg shape onto it.

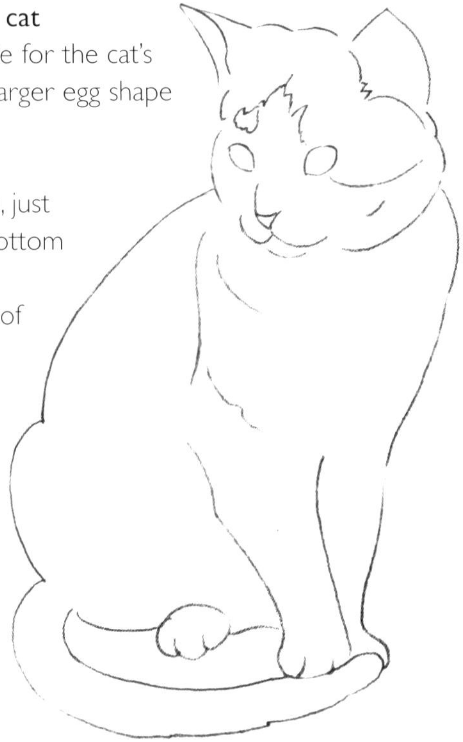

Join another circle, just overlapping the bottom of the egg shape. Then, at the base of this circle, add a much smaller circle for a paw. Dash in the curve to form the cat's back.

Add in two rectangular shapes for the front legs; see where they are positioned in relation to the egg shape and large circle shapes. Add two small circles for the front feet and dash in the tail, and also add in two triangles for the cat's ears.

Draw in the detail of the cat, removing the guidelines that you do not need.

Drawing Animals

Drawing a Horse

Firstly, draw an oval for the body with a large circle at both ends for the fore and rear quarters.

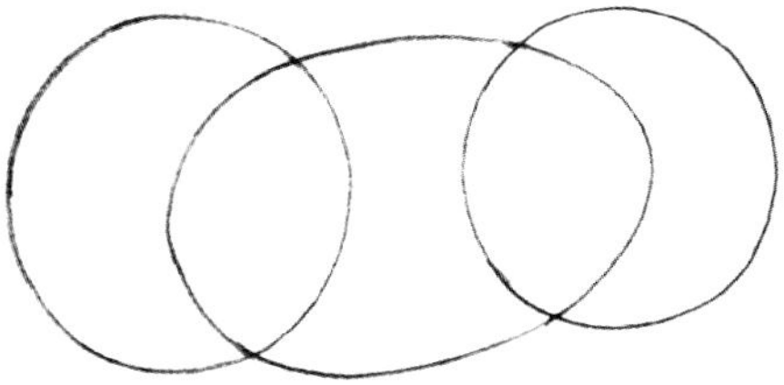

Make the neck and head by adding a cone with a circle just under the point and a small circle for the nose.

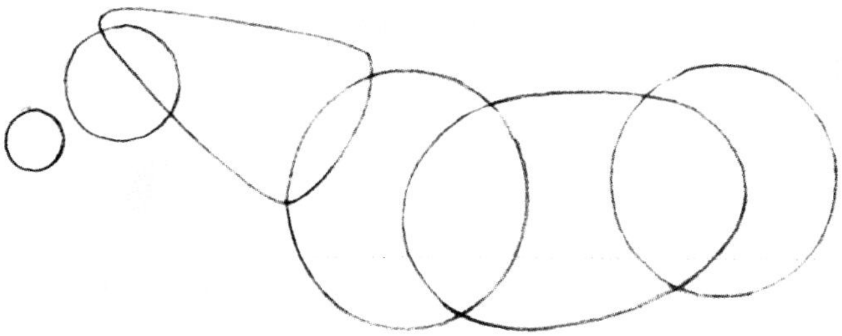

With a series of two sausage shapes and a rectangle draw in each of the legs. Add in the ears and connect the nose circle to the head circle.

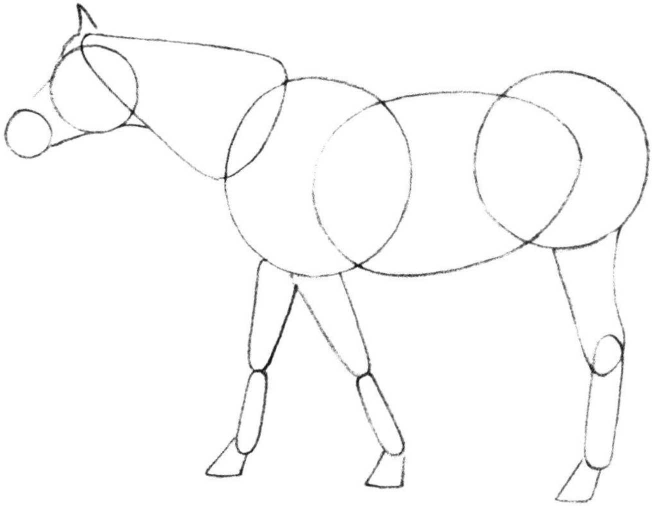

Draw in the detail of the horse, connecting all the shapes and add in its tail. Finally, remove all the guidelines that you no longer need.

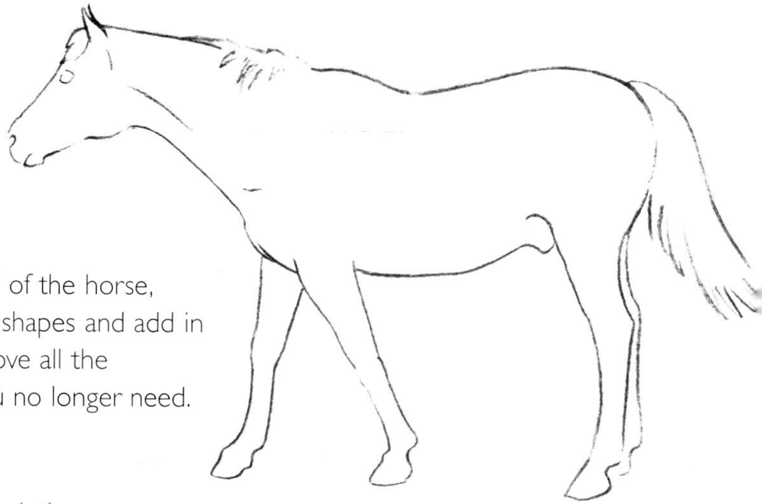

Drawing Animals

Drawing a Seated Dog

Start off with an angled, large, fat sausage shape for the main body. Onto the top of this, add a circle and, to that, a four-sided box shape.

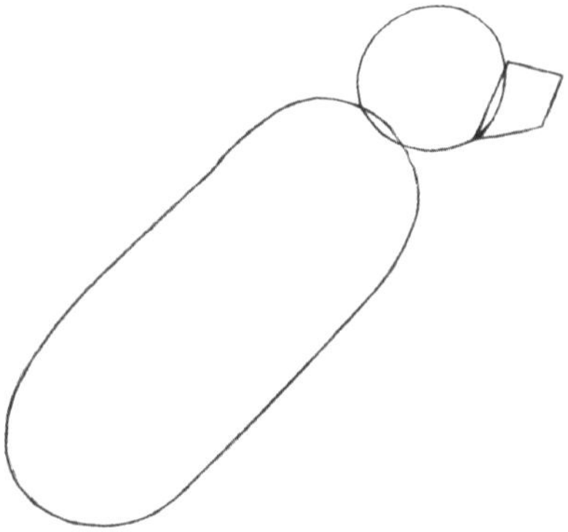

Within the bottom of the body shape, add an ovoid for the hunched up rear leg. Add a kite shape for the ear and a long sausage with a small sausage for the front leg, making sure the paws end up level with the bottom of the body.

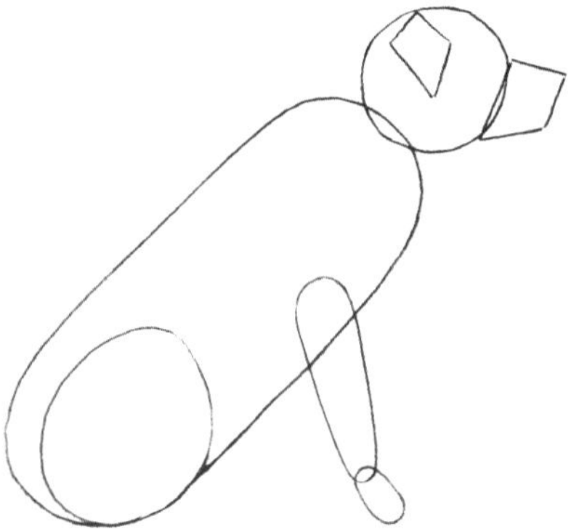

Add the shapes for the tail, rear leg, front paws, eye and the other front leg and paw.

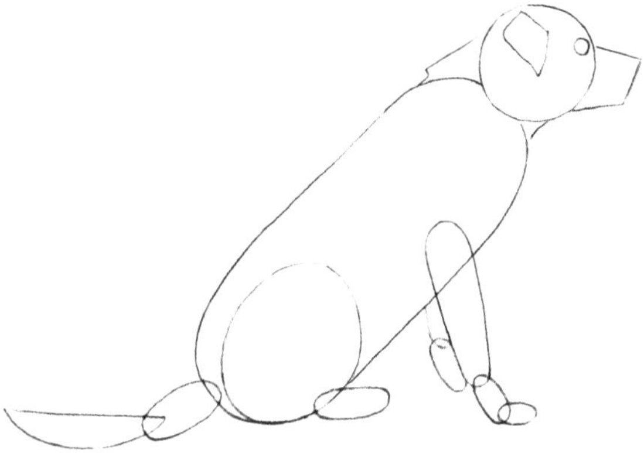

Connect up all the shapes and remove any unwanted guidelines.

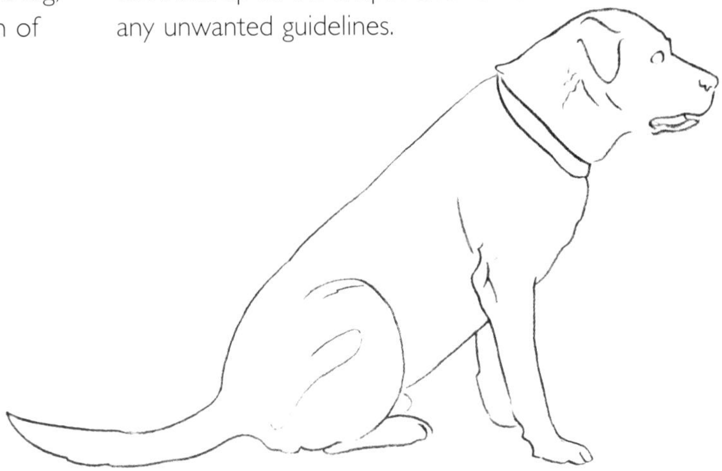

Drawing a Duckling

Firstly, draw an oval for the body and attach a smaller circle for the head.

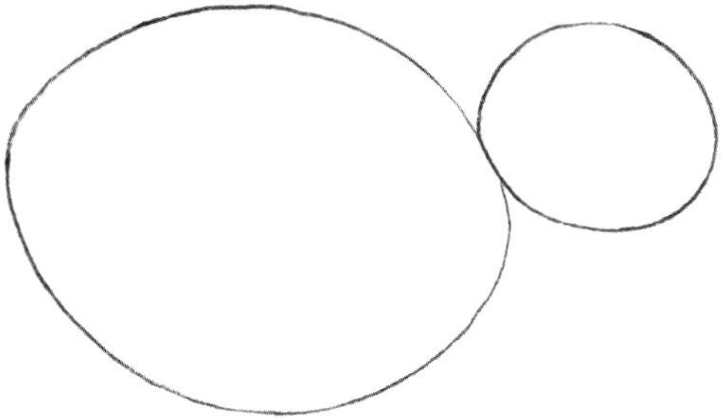

Add a rounded triangle to the rear of the body for the tail and one to the head for the beak.

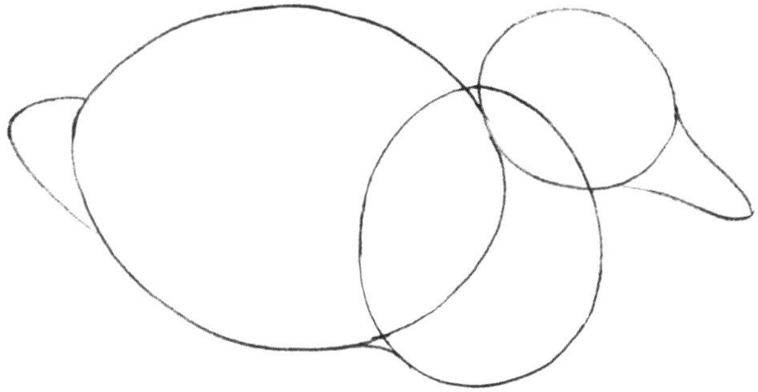

Add a middle-sized ovoid for the neck.

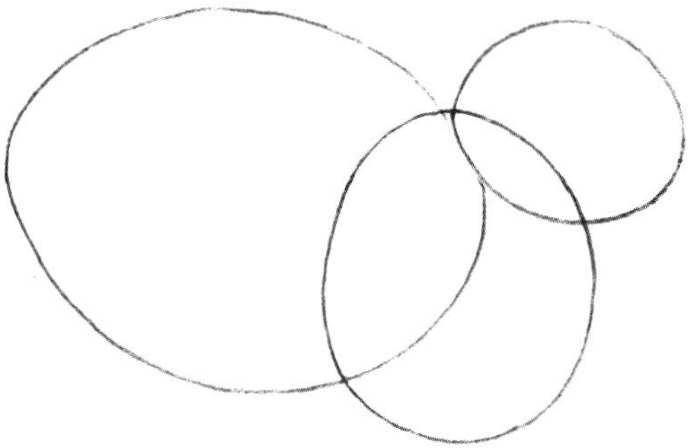

Draw in the detail of the duckling, connecting all the shapes and add in its legs and feet and eye.

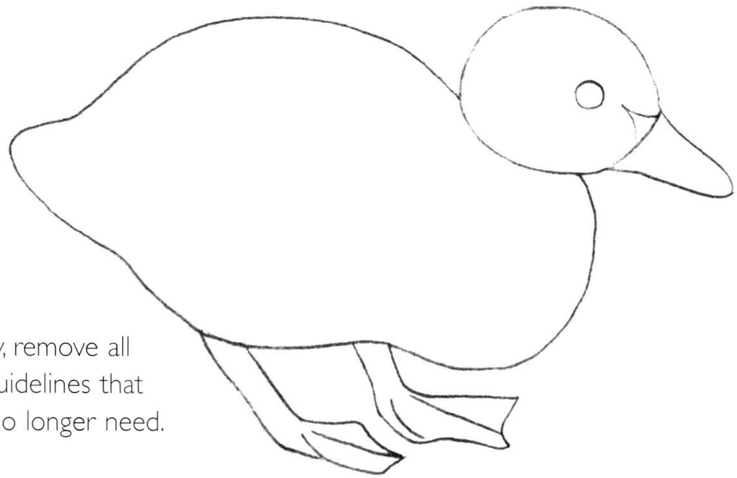

Finally, remove all the guidelines that you no longer need.

Drawing Animals

Practicality

Of course, the problem with painting animals is their tendency to move. One way to get round this is to paint from a photograph, but this method also has its disadvantages. When painting animals, you should strive to bring a sense of their vitality to your work and this is something likely to be lost in a photograph. Perhaps the best solution is to combine the two, sketching from life, but painting from a photograph.

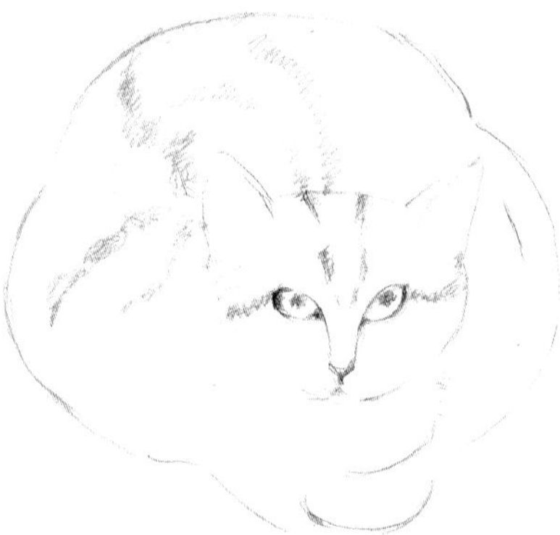

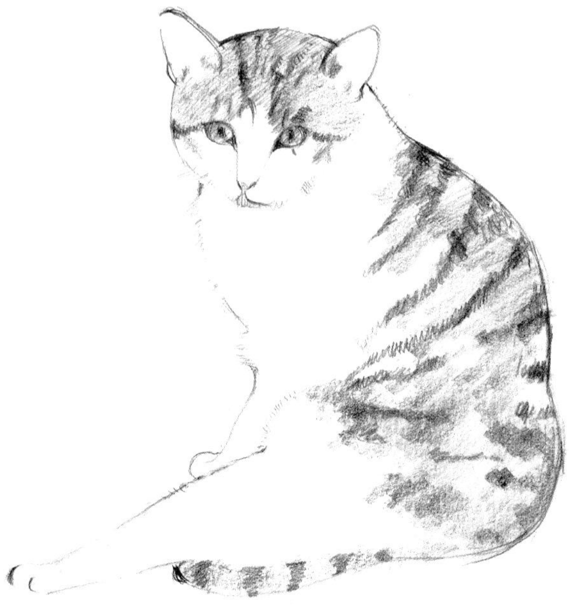

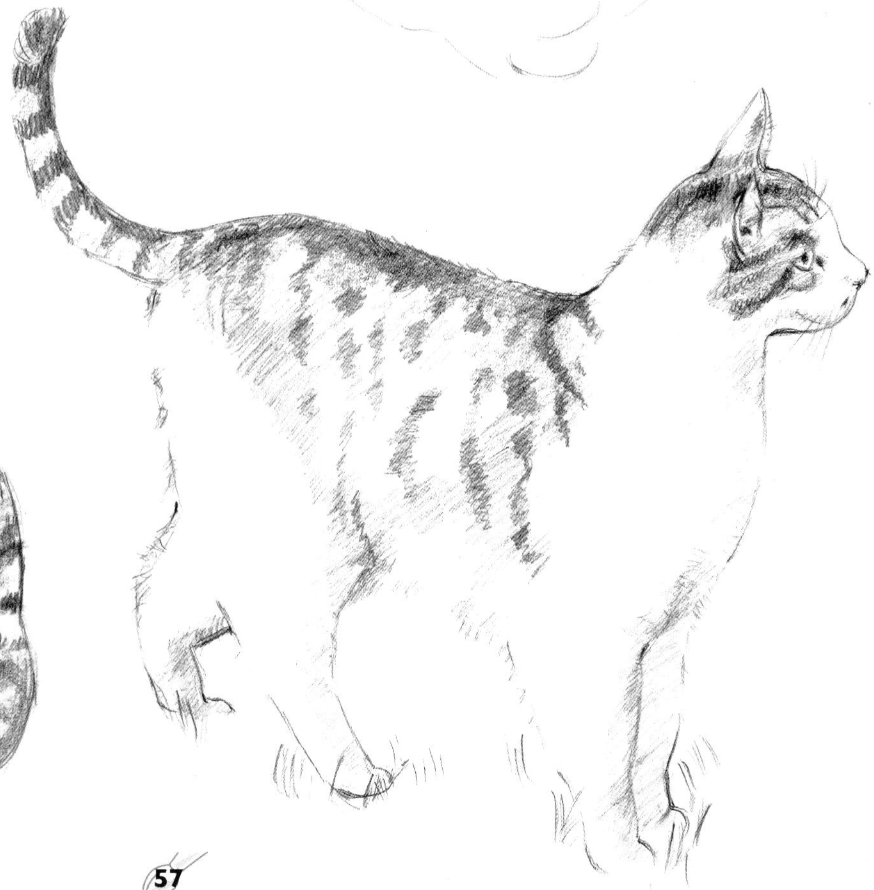

PROJECT SEVEN: Pet Portrait

As the cat is the main subject of this picture, the background has been kept simple. At first, the cat appears to be black, but on a closer inspection you will see that there is a range of rich colours which make up its fur.

1. Draw the outline of your picture, making sure not to press too hard; you need to see just enough of the outline. Once you have finished your painting and it is dry, you may rub off any heavy lines.

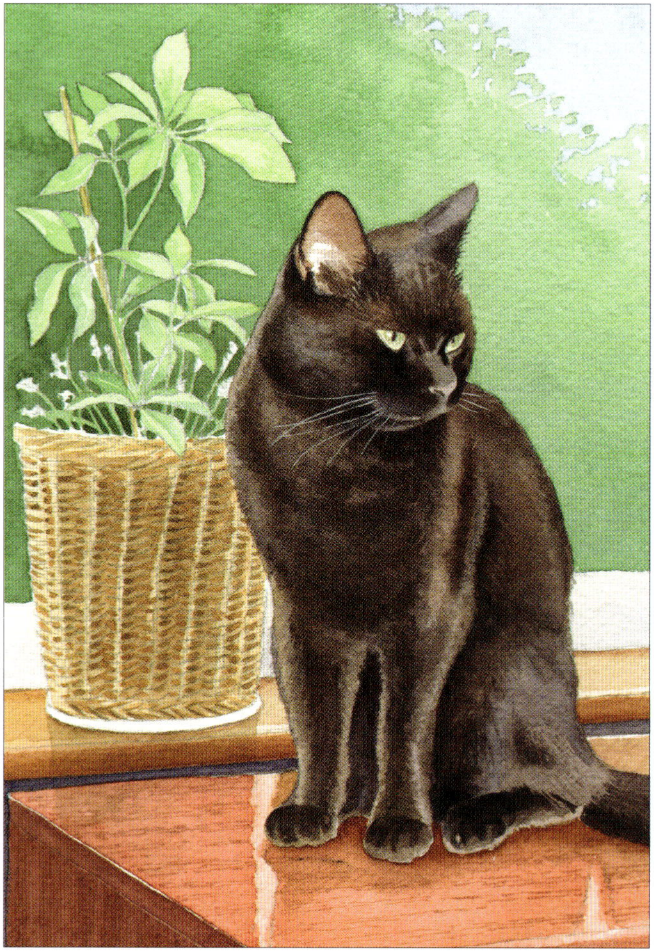

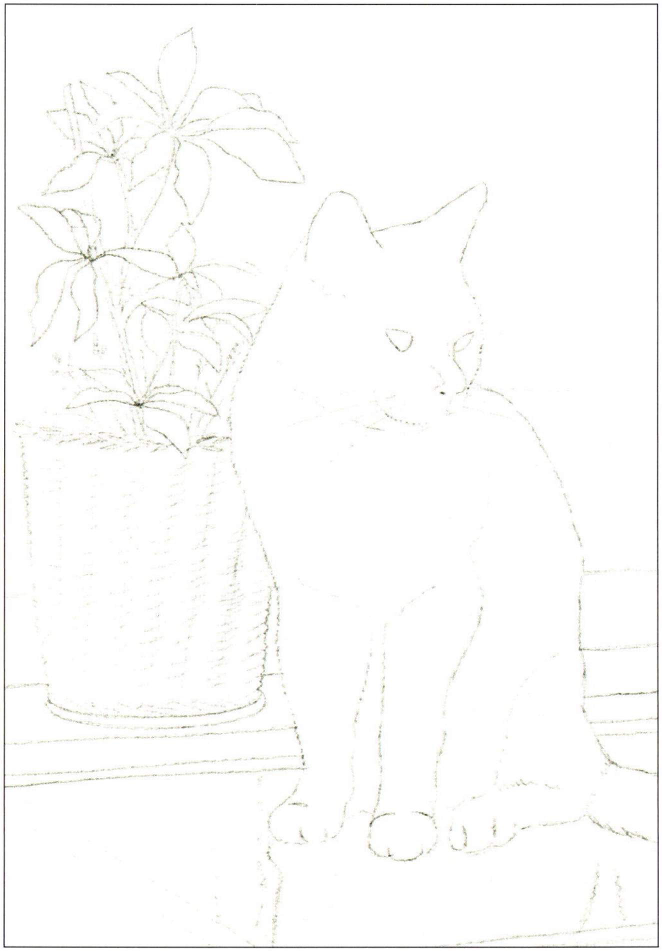

Pet Portrait

2. Wet the paper where the background colour is required. Mix a sufficient quantity of sap green, ultramarine and a small amount of alizarin crimson and paint the background an even, flat wash. Do the same for the corner of sky. Wash over the cabinets using alizarin crimson and burnt sienna, leaving the areas of highlights. Once dried, repaint the cabinets with the same colour.

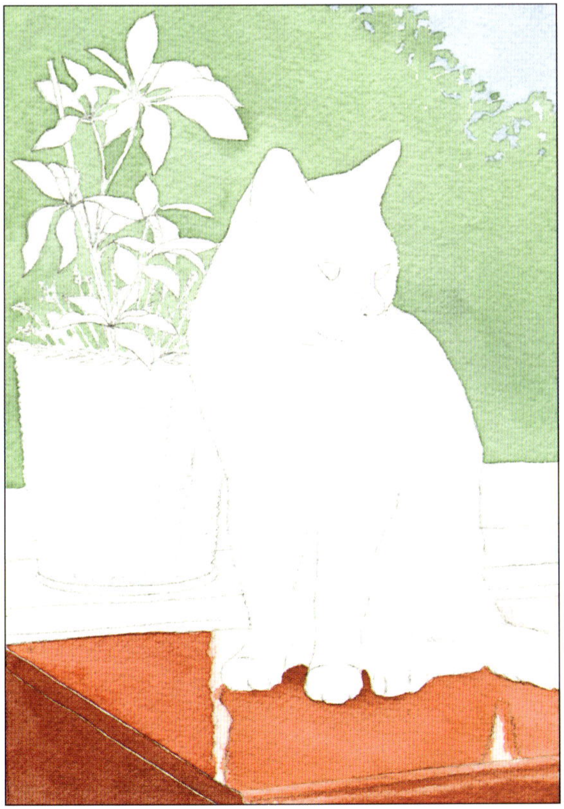

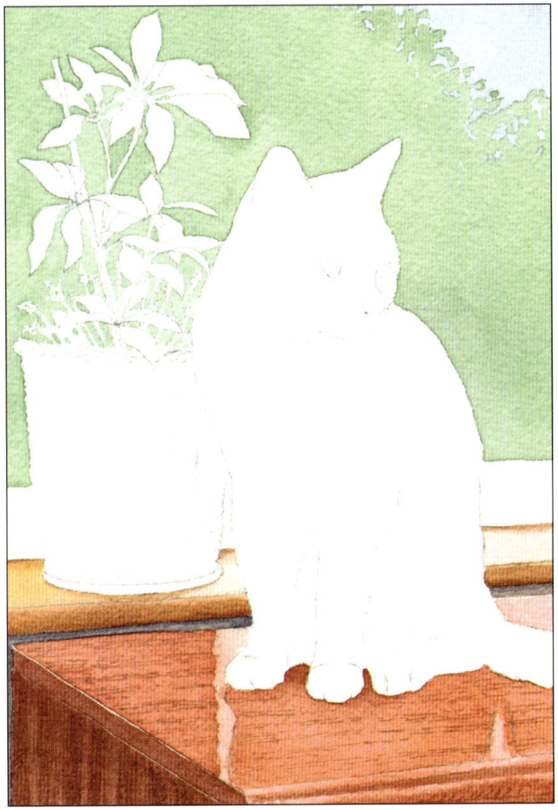

3. Wet the paper and apply a mix of burnt sienna, yellow ochre and ultramarine to the darkest areas of the windowsill; the paint will fade into the lighter areas. As the paper dries, keep dropping in more colour to strengthen the areas where darker tones are needed. Using a dry-on-dry technique, add the grain to the cabinet with long, thin strokes of ultramarine and alizarin crimson.

Pet Portrait

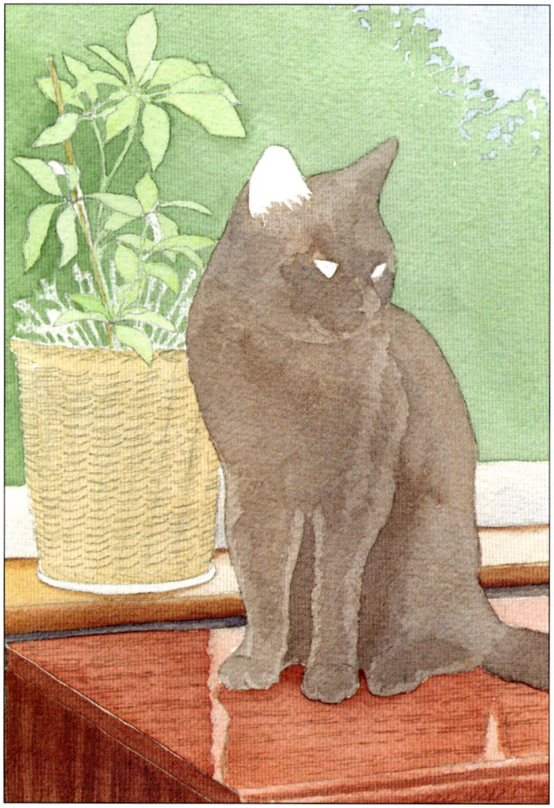

4. Paint the foliage of the plant with sap green and lemon yellow. Add the window frame with a mix of ultramarine, burnt sienna and alizarin crimson. Redefine the drawing of the basket and apply an even coat of burnt sienna and yellow ochre. Make a soft brown from ultramarine, burnt sienna and alizarin crimson and apply over the whole cat apart from its eyes and the inside of its ear.

5. Once the paint has dried, use exactly the same mixture for the darker areas to start layering and building up the cat's form. Intensify the darker tones by a succession of layers. Keep the paper wet to make the colours soft and to avoid hard edges (brushstrokes should be in the same direction as the fur) to add definition.

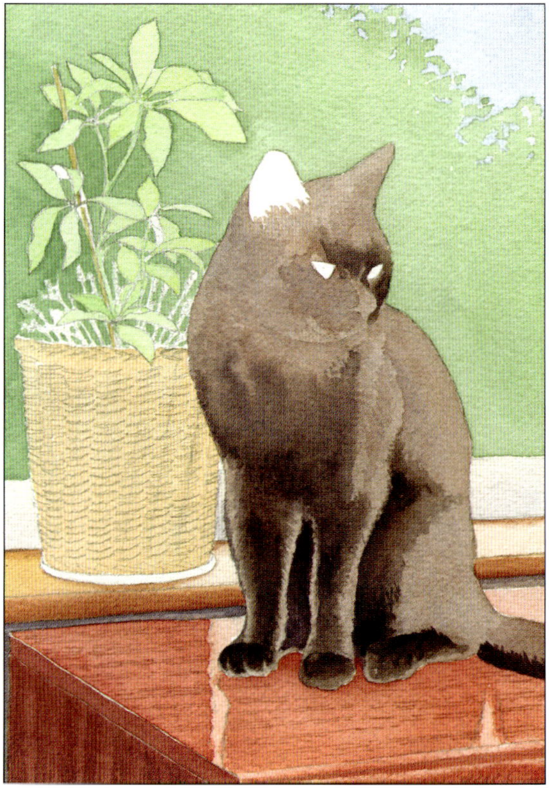

Pet Portrait

6. Carry on intensifying the darker tones of the cat, adding more ultramarine or alizarin crimson to achieve the full range of colours in the fur. Mix lemon yellow and sap green for the cat's eyes. Once dried, add the pupils with a mix of ultramarine and alizarin crimson. Then, use alizarin crimson to paint the inside of the ear. Before the paint dries, lift out the colour where there are highlights in the ear.

7. Mix three varying shades of yellow ochre, raw sienna and ultramarine for the range of tones in the basket. Pick out the patterns of light and dark in the weave. Intensify the colour background to bring the foliage plant forward. Use white paint and a very fine brush to add the cat's whiskers.

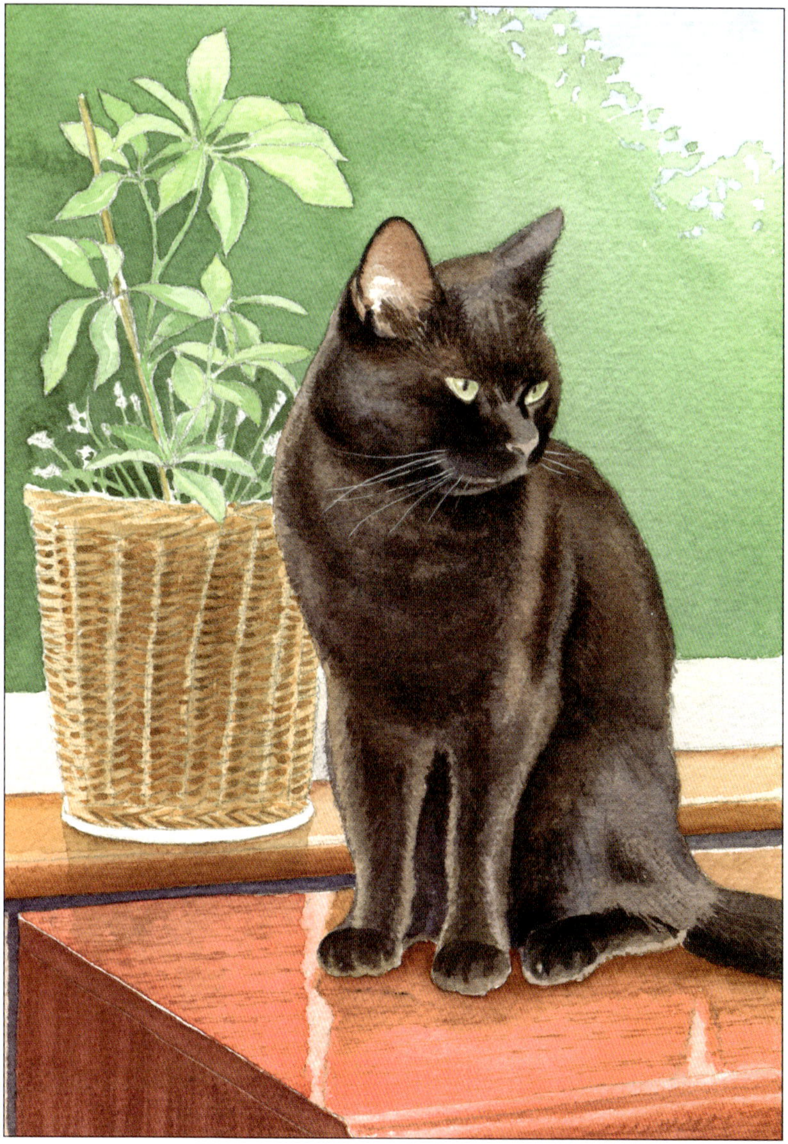

PROJECT EIGHT: Horse

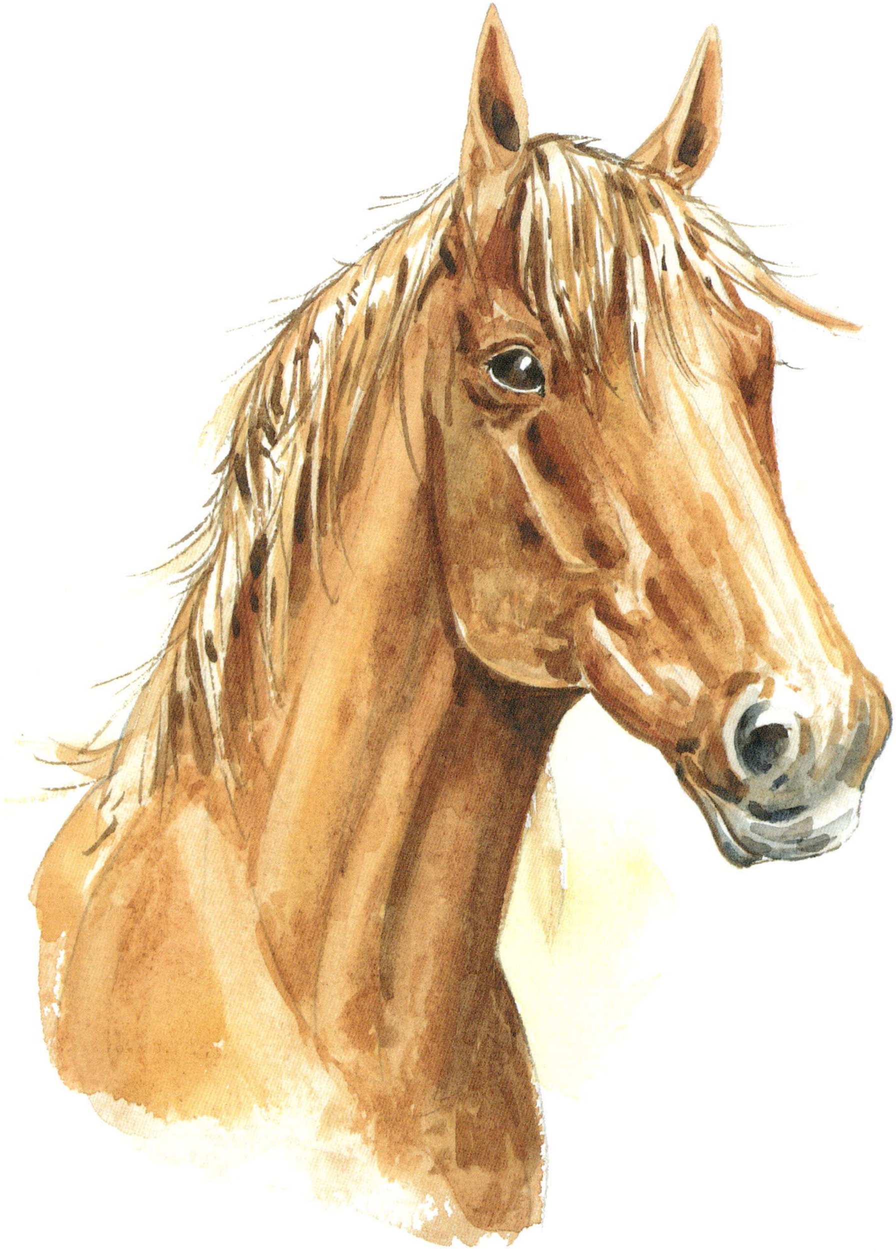

Horse

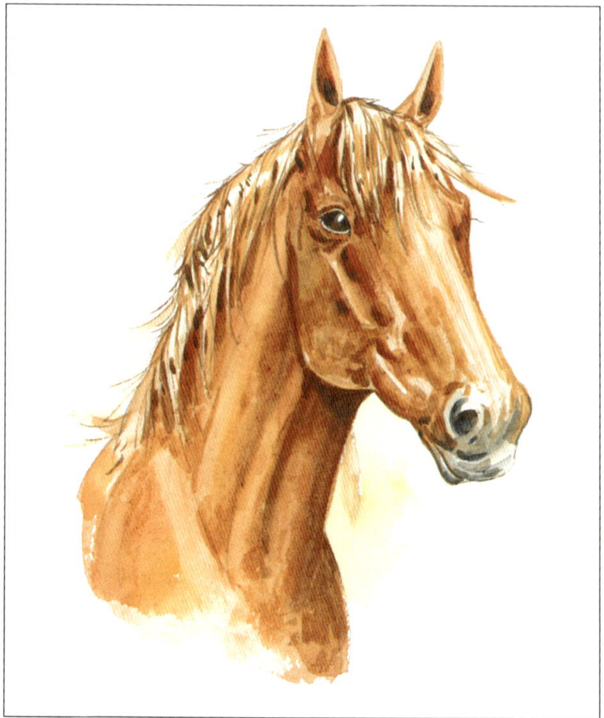

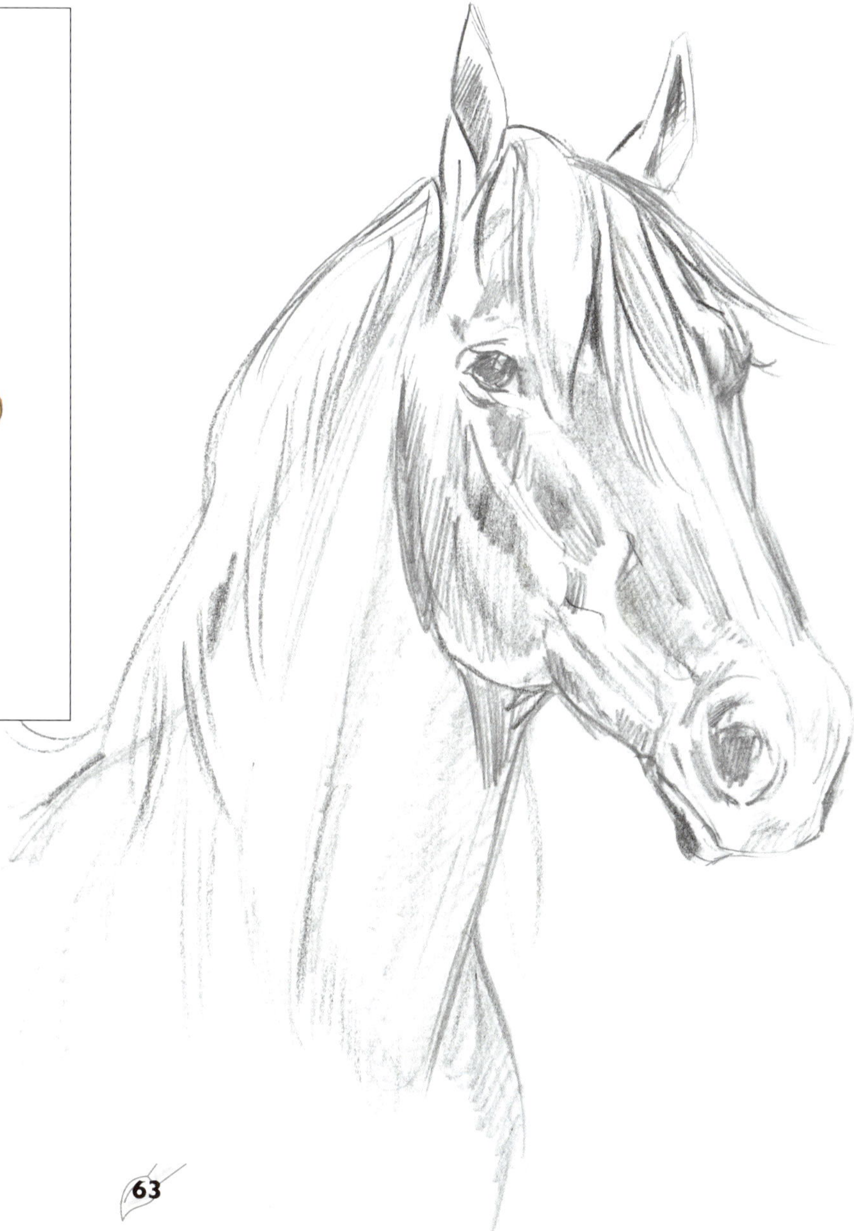

Horses are a wonderful subject for animal lovers. A good painting can bring out the essential character of the animal.

Horse

1. Sketch or trace the line drawing on page 93. The close-up detail here can be used to establish tonal values. Use a pencil for the main shapes, making sure you give due consideration to where the light is coming from and where the highlights are to fall on your subject.

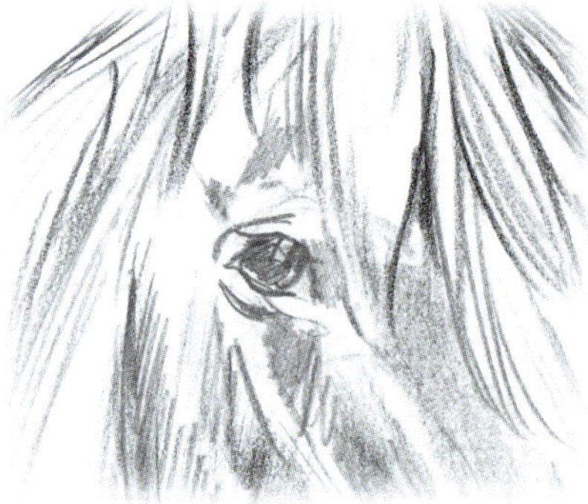

2. Paint the eye with a grey wash, reserving the white highlight. This should bring a dark grey/black shape to the eye. Next, use a light brown to fill the majority of the eye, then sweep a curving wash of dark brown in the eye, as shown.

Although the horse's eye forms only a small proportion of the painting, getting it right is crucial to the quality of the finished picture.

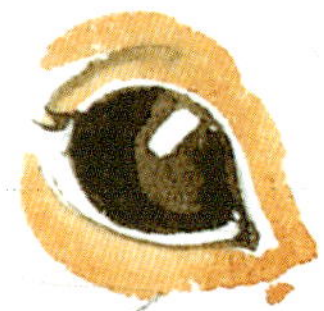

3. For the colour of the horse's mane and ears, begin with a brown-red wash. While the wash is still wet, remove some of the paint with a dry brush rinsed in clean water. This will lift off the colour, helping to bring vitality to the mane. Continue to build colour with different shades of brown.

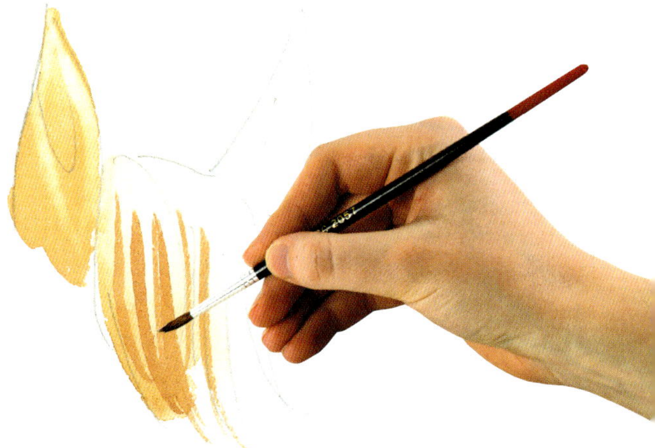

Use a dry brush rinsed in clean water to lift off colour.

Horse

4. Work in the opposite manner for the area around the horse's nose. Build up the colour with progressively darker colours – this will help you to create shape, giving definition to the nose.

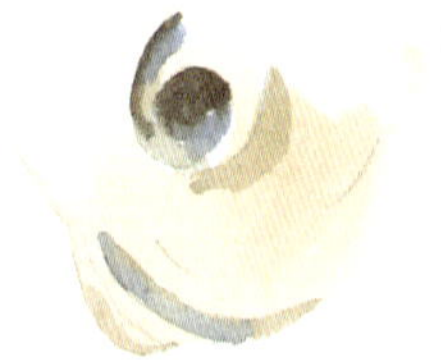

Start with a light wash for the horse's nose.

5. Apply a light brown wash to the horse's body, then remove the areas you want to stay lighter with a paper towel. Add definition to the horse's form by applying progressively darker colours. Continue using a dabbing technique to leave a texture.

Create highlights by removing the wash while still wet with a paper towel.

6. After working the colour into the horse's mane (step 3), finish the impression of hair by adding a fine line with a rigger brush. Add a pale wash of colour to the background to finish.

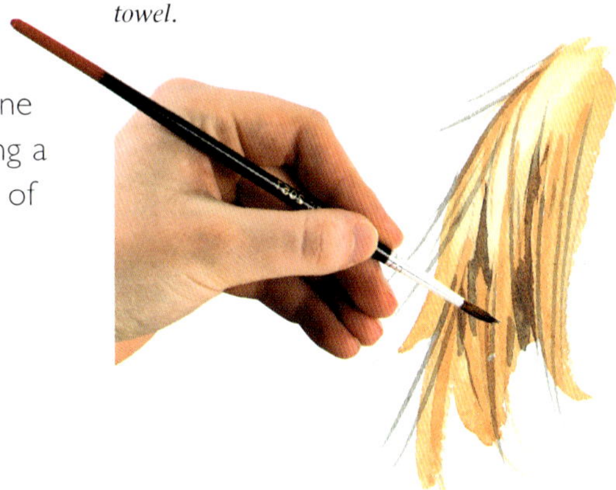

After working the colour into the horse's mane, finish the impression of hair with a rigger brush.

Basic Anatomy

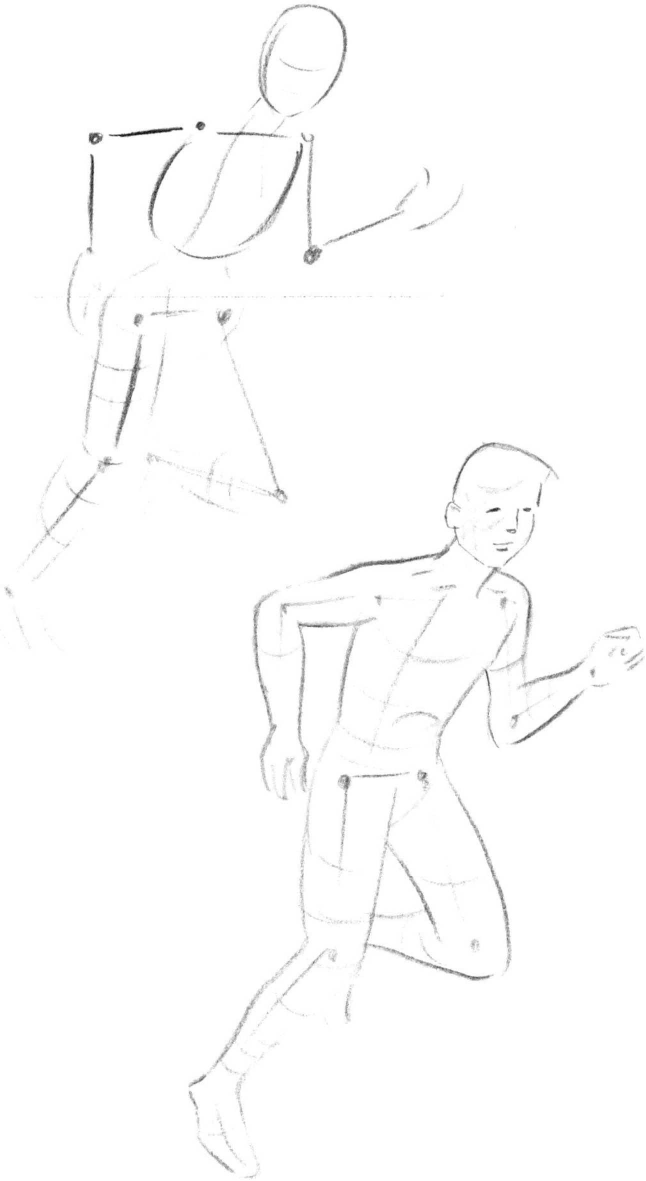

1. The line and dot technique is a simple method to draw the human form. Begin by drawing a stick figure. Draw a small dot at the point of each body joint.

2. Now, draw a stick figure in an action pose. You will need to take into account the body's centre of gravity, which is typically located just below the belly button. The relationship of the centre of gravity to the body's 'resting points' will dictate the sense of movement.

3. The stick figure establishes the figure's proportions. Now, join up the dots with cylinder shapes to give the figure its body. Note that the legs (at the waist) are roughly half the total height of the figure and that, with the arm hanging freely, the bottom of the hand comes about halfway down the thigh.

4. Smooth out the cylinder shapes to give the impression of muscles and clothing.

Basic Anatomy

The Head

5. The head is usually approximately one-seventh the size of the body. However, bear in mind when drawing from life that body shape varies from person to person. The head will also be one-third the width of the shoulders. The proportions of the head itself are broken up into separate areas. The top of the head to the eyebrow line forms one part, the eyebrow line to below the nose another part and from the bottom of the nose to the chin another. There are two further subdivisions, the eyeline and the mouthline.

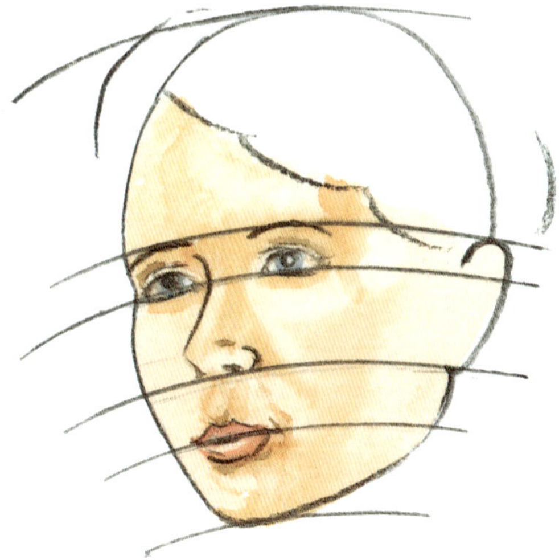

The distance from the nose line to the eyebrows and from the nose line to the bottom of the chin is roughly the same. The distance from the eye line to the bottom of the chin and from the eye line to the top of the head is roughly similar. The ear should extend from the nose line to the eyebrow line.

6. Not only should you use horizontal guidelines for the head you should use vertical ones as well. Two vertical lines drawn up from the lips should touch the inside of each iris. Vertical lines within the lip lines should mark out the width of the nose.

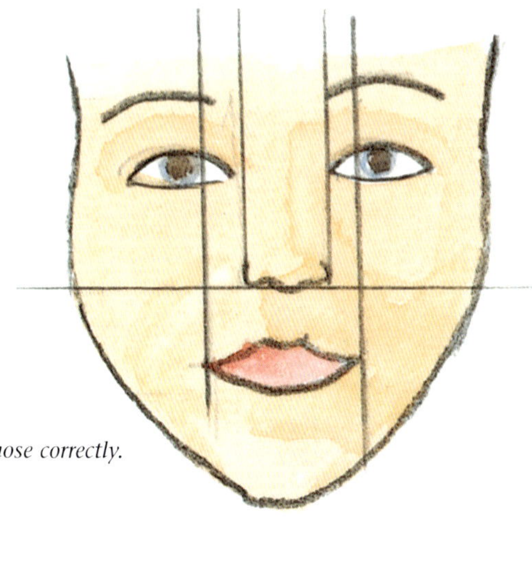

Use guidelines to position the lips and nose correctly.

Arms and Legs

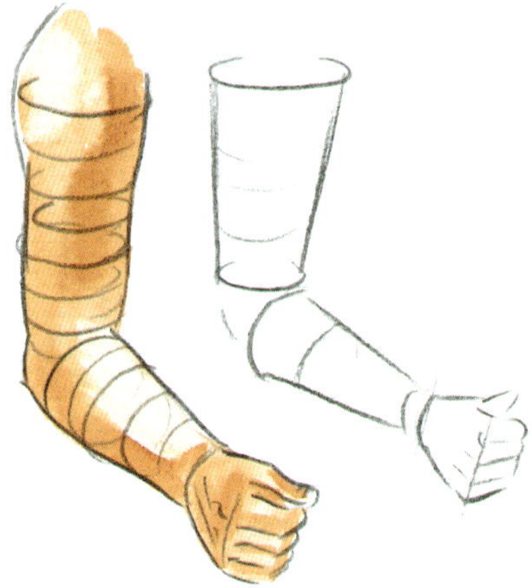

7. The arm is drawn in three cylinder shapes: the upper arm, the lower arm and the hand. The hand should be approximately one-third the length of the arm. When drawing arms in great detail, it is worth remembering that there are three main bones: the radius, the ulna and the humerus.

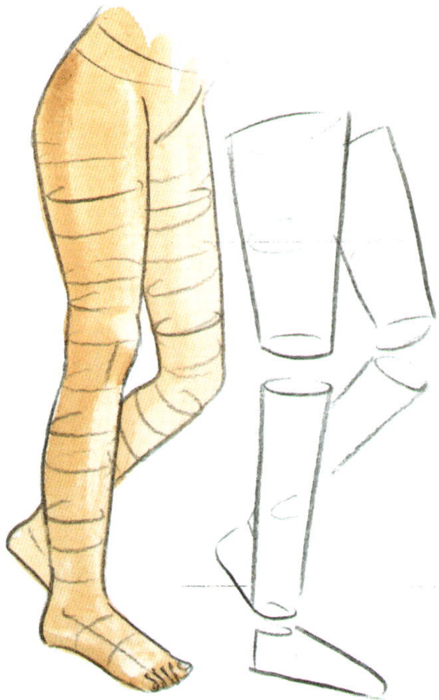

8. You should approach the legs in the same way that you approach the other parts of the body, by breaking them down into simple geometric shapes. As with the arm, the leg should be divided into three cylindrical shapes, one for the upper leg, one for the lower leg and one for the foot. The key to success when drawing anatomical figures is always to break them down into more manageable shapes.

Basic Anatomy

Hands and Feet

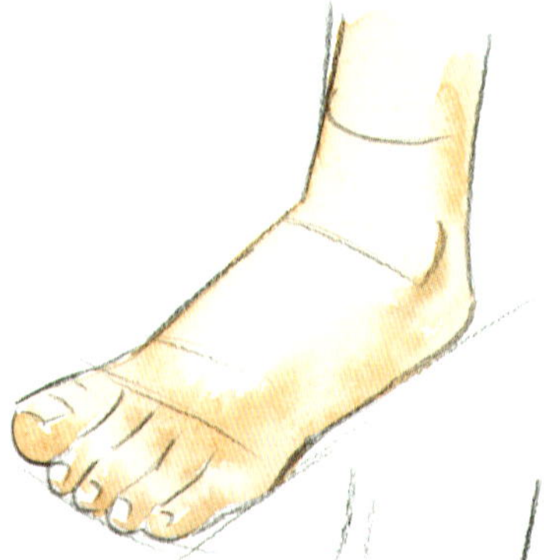

9. Hands and feet are notoriously difficult to draw but they needn't be. Draw a box-like shape to establish the foot's form and proportion. As with hands to arms, feet will be one-third the length of the legs. Although the head is divided into halves, most other proportions work in thirds.

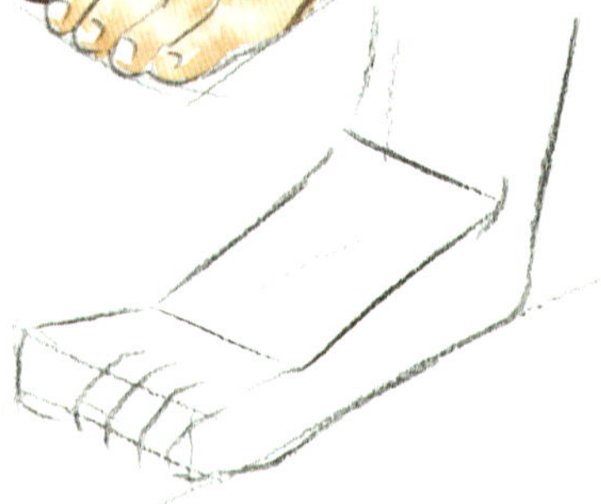

10. Smooth out the box shape to give detail to the foot.

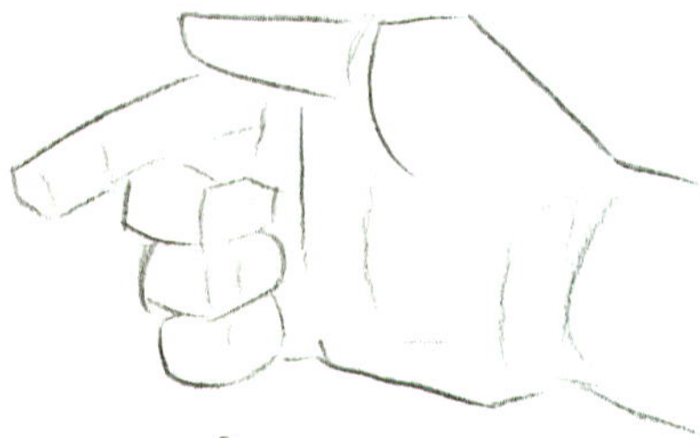

11. Use the same technique for the hands. Draw a box-like shape to establish form and proportion, then smooth out the box shape to give detail. Never overwork the details of feet or hands as they can look laboured and draw away attention from what may be otherwise a good-quality painting. Treat them sympathetically, but always keep them simple.

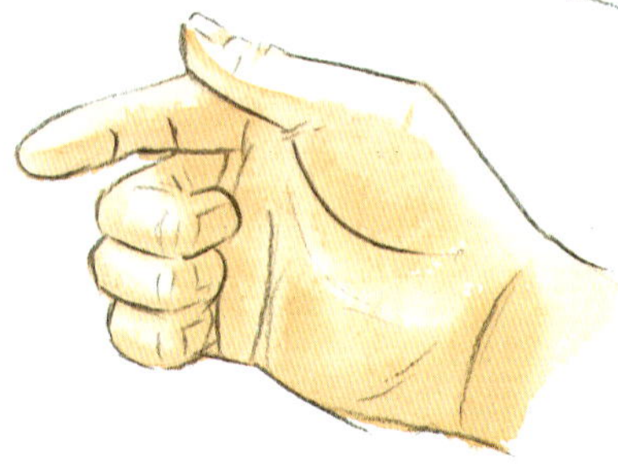

Basic Anatomy

The human figure can be divided into six separate parts, all of similar proportions to one another apart from the feet division which is smaller. Dividing the body up in this way will help you to keep the figure in correct proportion.

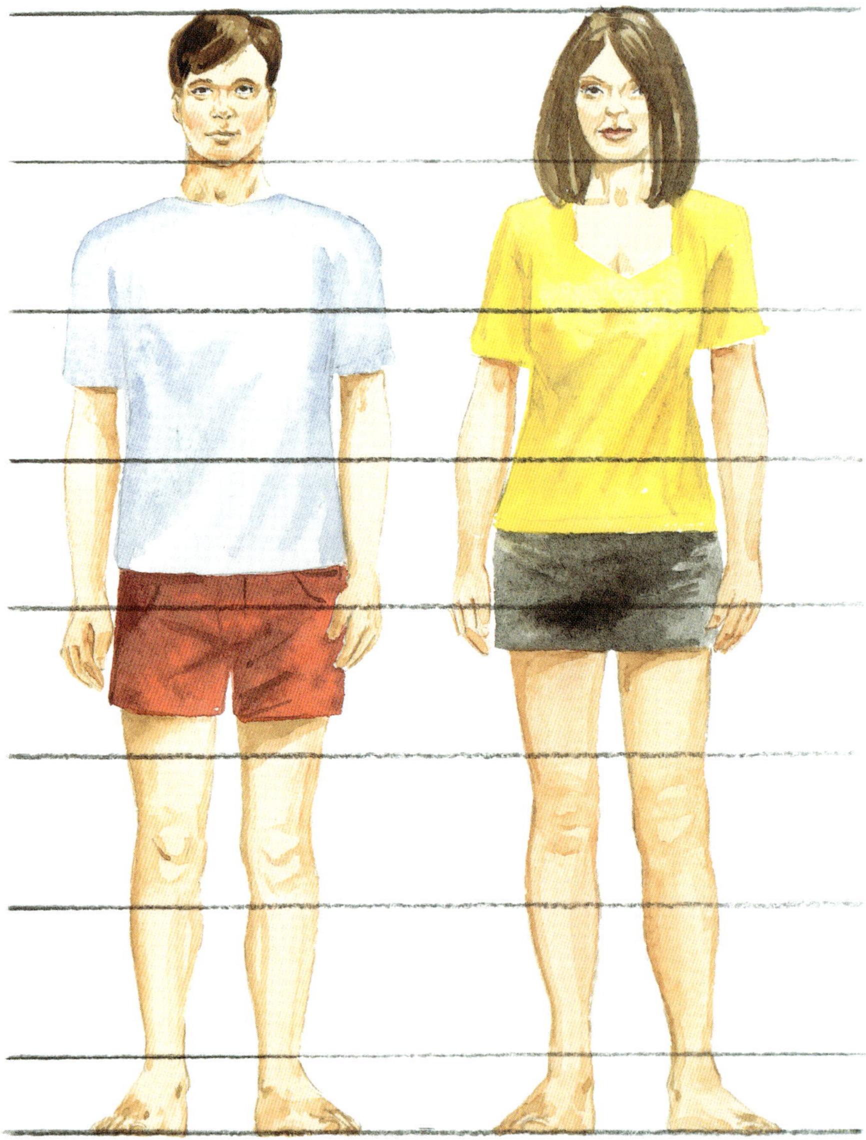

Basic Anatomy

Faces are interesting to draw; they can be studied from many angles, each providing the artist with challenges. The most important thing is to examine and observe your model.

Start your portrait with a large upside down egg shape. Most faces fit this basic shape. Take this shape and divide it vertically and horizontally. The vertical line will be the centre of the face and on top of the horizontal centre line place the two eyes. The space between the eyes is normally the width of one eye and eyes should be oval in shape. Divide the bottom half of the oval again and estimate from your model where the mouth should be in relation to this imaginary line.

Look at the mouth and see where it finishes in relation to the eyes and draw down lines from the eyes. Do the same for the width of the nose.

The tops of the ears should also be drawn by looking at their position in relation to the eyes and the earlobes in relation to the mouth. Draw in the hair, neck, and eyebrows and rub out the guidelines. Alter the shape of the oval to suit the chin.

Lastly, remember that faces are not symmetrical so look for the differences from one side of the face to the other.

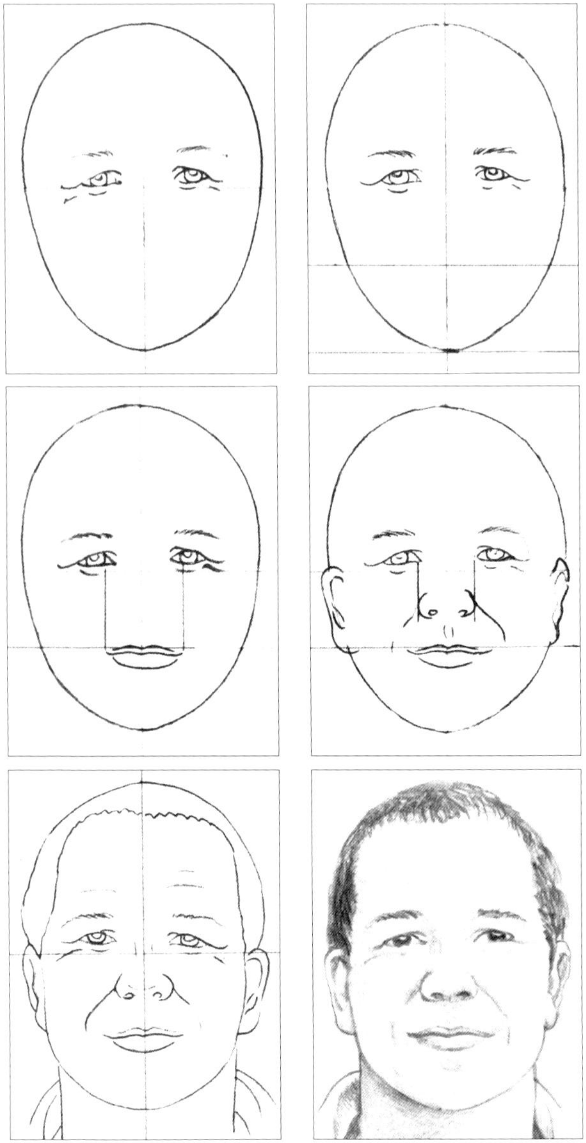

Basic Anatomy

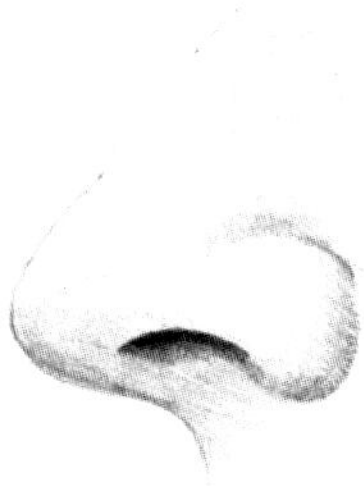

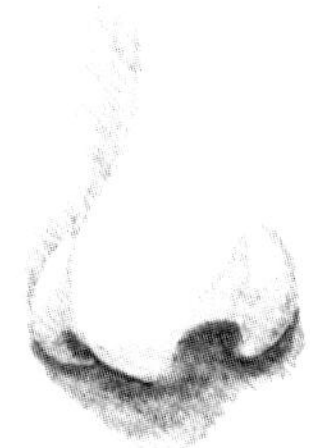

In order to get a good likeness, it is essential to get the position, size and shape of all the features in relation to each other. These rules also apply from the side, as well as from other angles.

Noses

Noses change depending on the angle from which they are viewed. From the front, the shape is defined mostly by shading, but from the side they need more lines to define them.

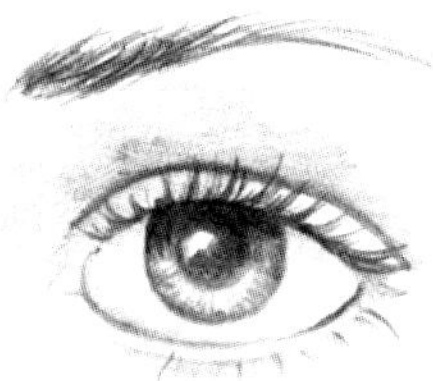

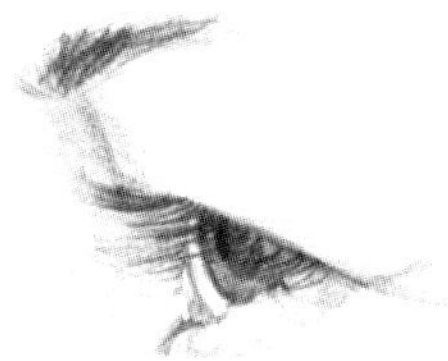

Eyes

The eyes are often the focal point of the portrait and are usually what gives it life. Eyes are complex in shape and to capture them will often lead to a successful portrait.

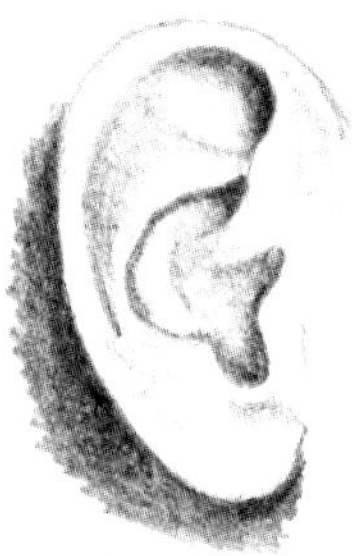

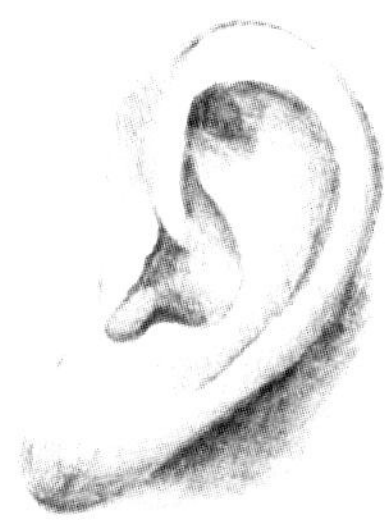

Ears

Ears are always different in shape from face to face. The lobes in particular differ in size and shape so careful observation is required.

Mouths

Mouths are interesting and change with facial expressions. They can be open or closed. Keep the lines of lips soft.

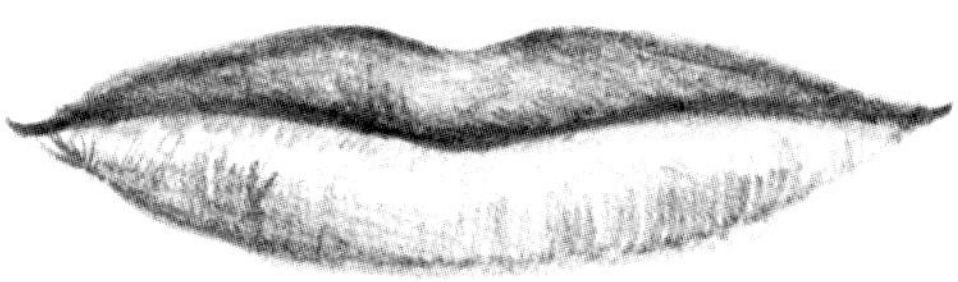

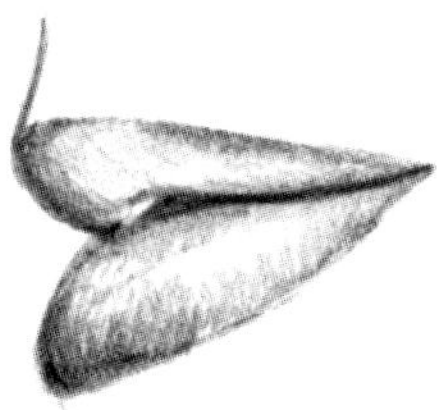

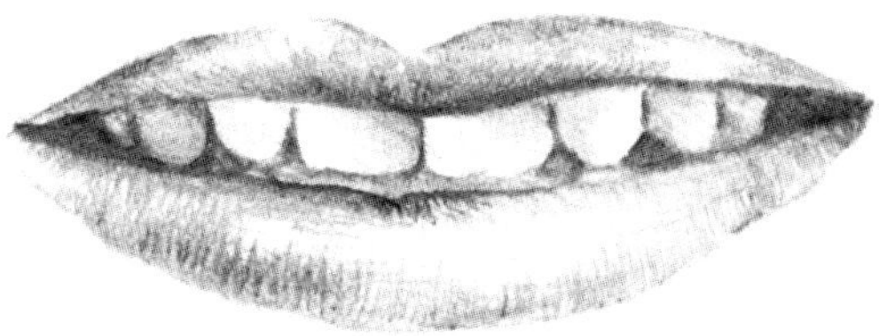

PROJECT NINE: Portrait Study

This portrait captures the fresh look of a young face on a windswept beach. The background is a simple series of washes of the sea.

1. Lightly sketch your picture, being careful not to put too much pencil on the painting surface as this can leave unwanted grey marks.

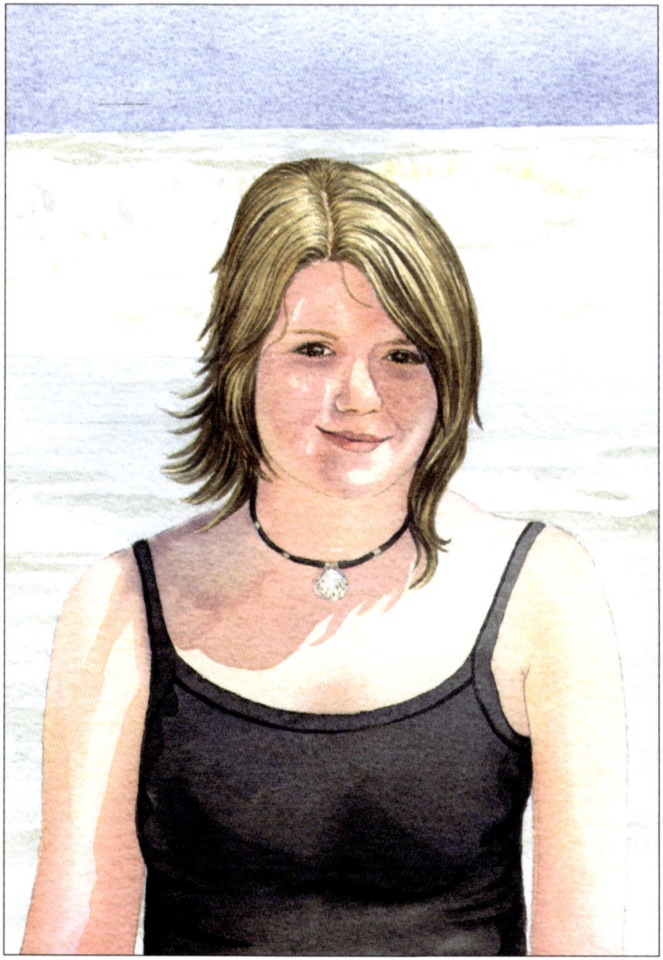

Portrait Study

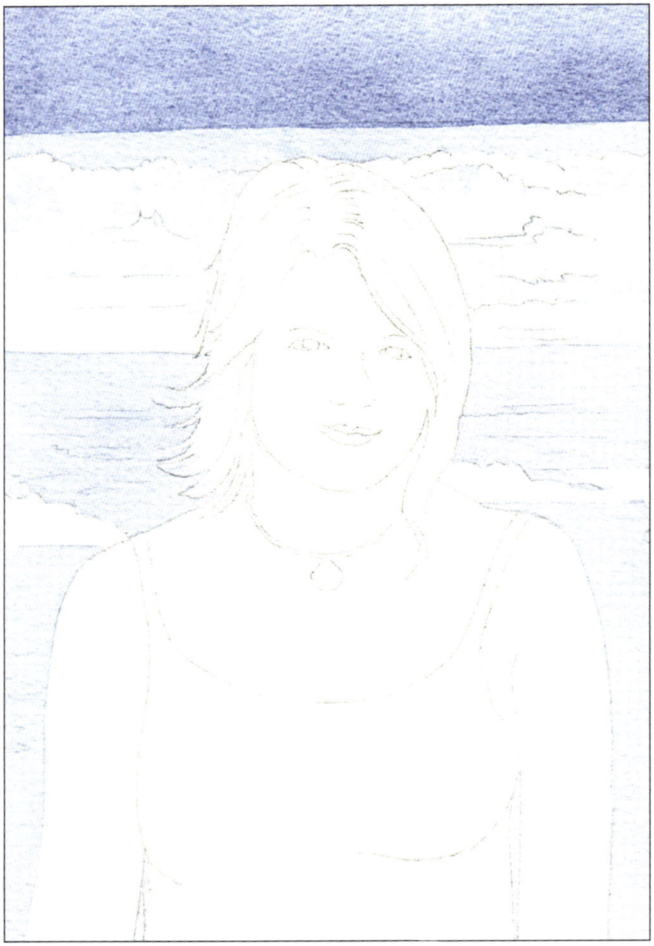

2. In your palette, make up a dilute ultramarine. Wet the sky area with clean water and apply an ultramarine wash. When that has dried, use an even more dilute wash to paint the blue parts of the sea.

3. Mix a pale wash of yellow ochre and alizarin crimson. Wet the entire skin area, including the eyes, and apply the skin tone. Try to make the wash for the skin tone even and consistent.

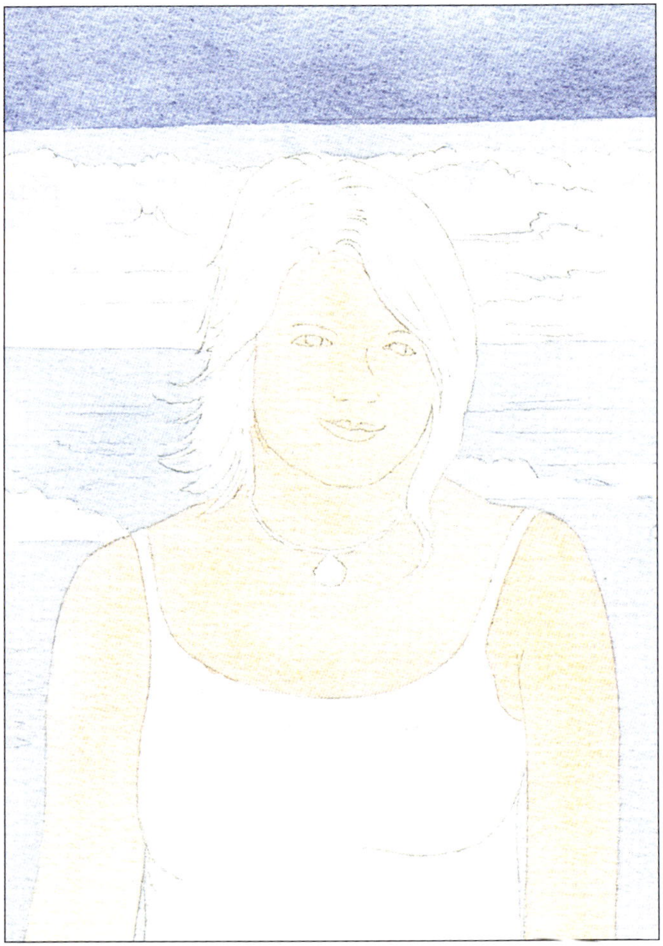

Portrait Study

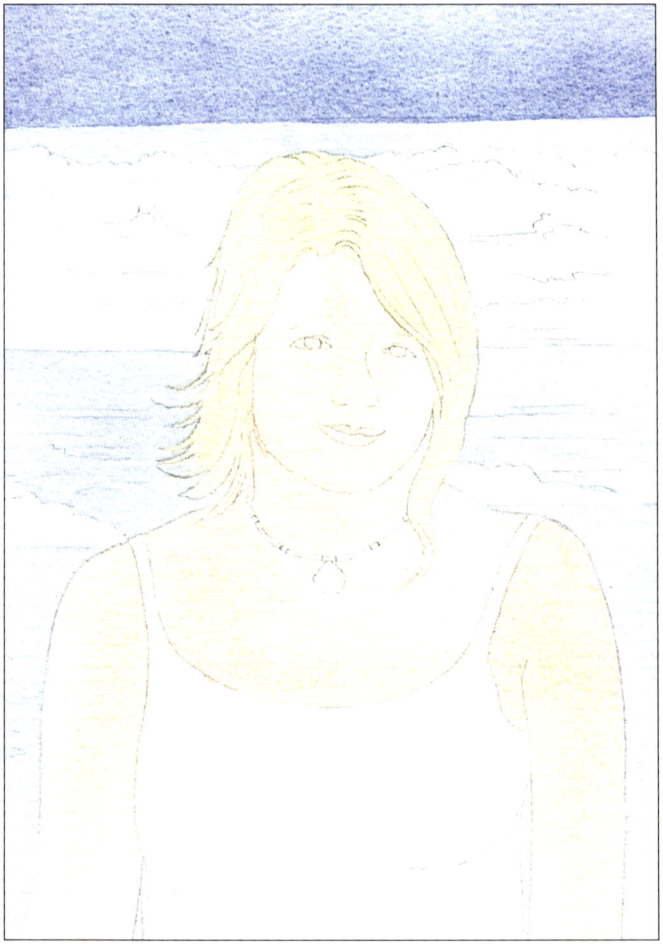

4. Use a pale wash of yellow ochre for the base colour of the hair.

5. For the top, make a wash from ultramarine and burnt sienna. You will need more ultramarine if the mix is not dark enough. Again, wet the area before painting to ensure you get an even wash.

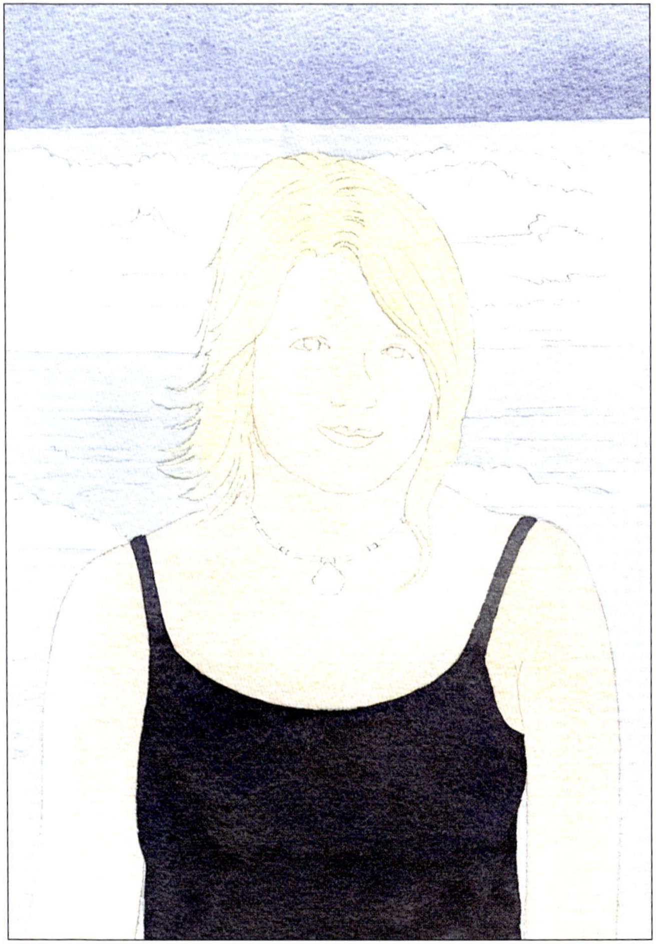

6. Make up a darker skin tone from alizarin crimson and yellow ochre for the shadows. You don't need to wet the paper before you paint this time because some of the shadows (especially on the chest) have hard edges. The shadows which do have softer edges will need softening with a clean, wet paintbrush.

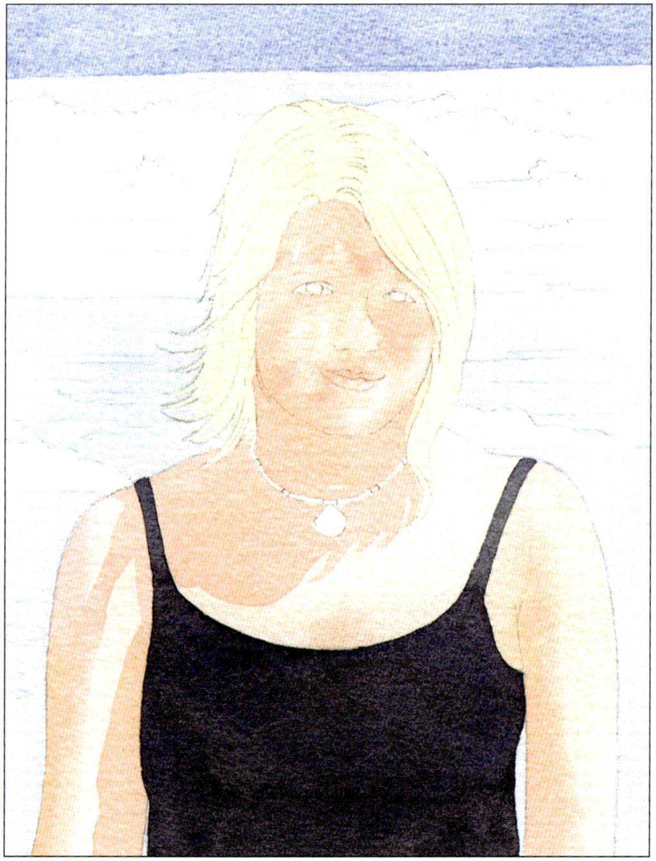

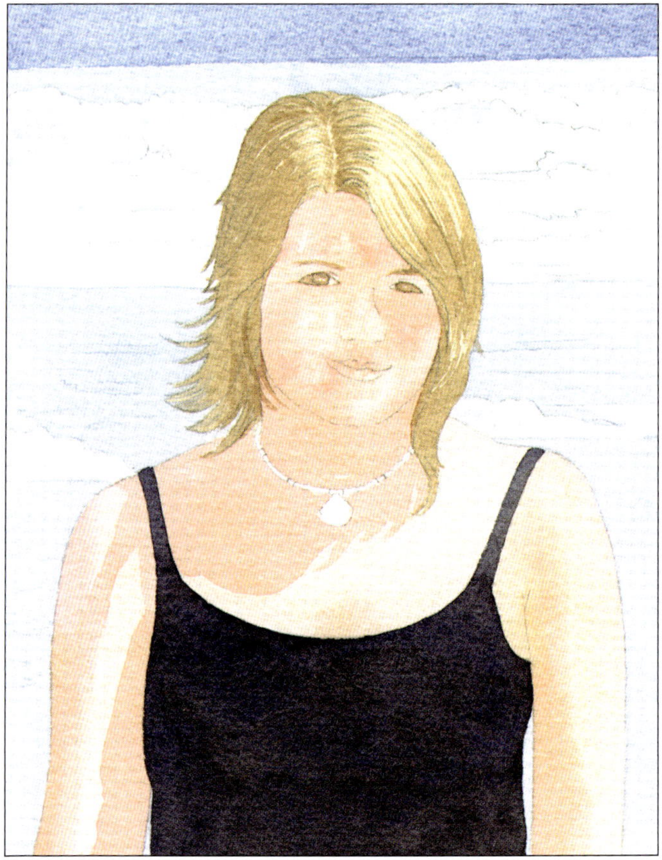

7. Mix up a brown with burnt sienna and ultramarine and lighten it with some yellow ochre. Paint in all the darker hair, leaving the highlights clean. With this darker tone, add in the eyebrows, irises and eyelashes.

Portrait Study

8. Make the brown mix a bit darker with some more ultramarine and add some darker areas to the hair and eyes, this time leaving out the eyebrows. Remember to paint in the direction of the hair strands, as this will inject more life into the piece.

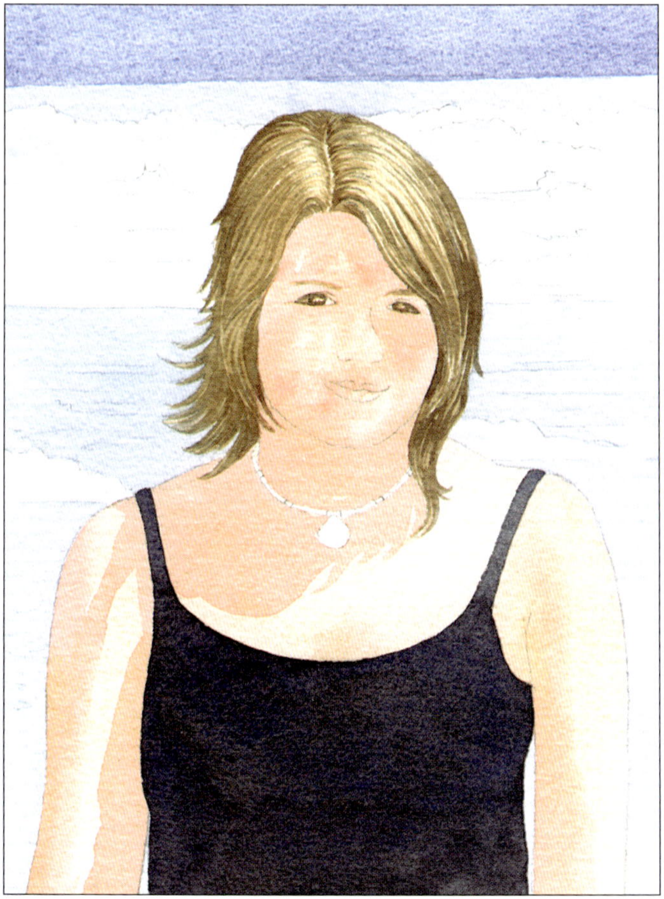

9. Mix up a pale wash of alizarin crimson and ultramarine and apply them to the face, leaving the lighter areas. Pink up the sides of the neck and soften the edges. Then, apply pink shadows to the chest and arms. Make up a redder mix for the lips; making sure to leave some areas lighter.

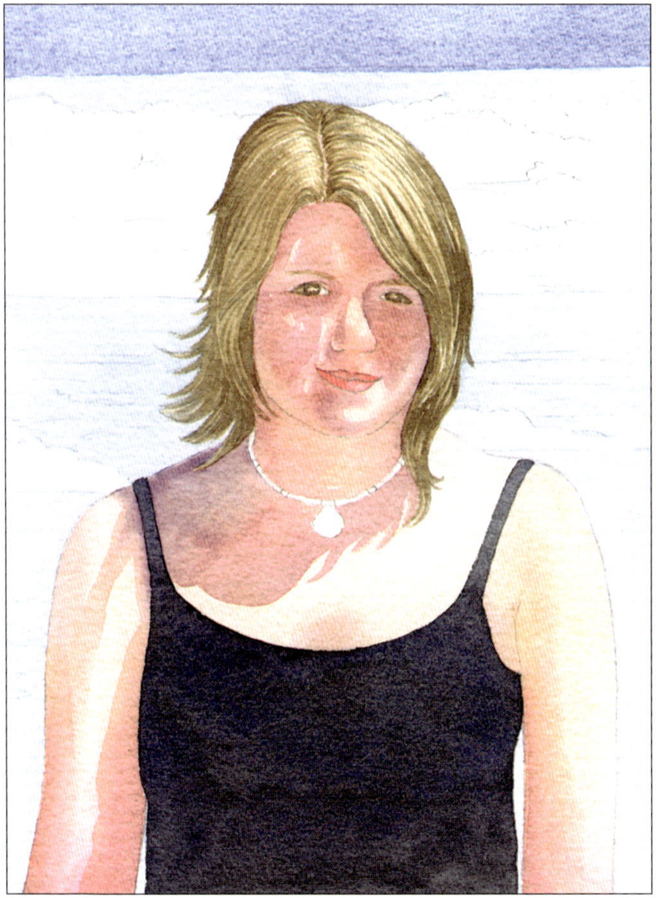

Portrait Study

10. With the darker skin tones in place, the hair needs more definition. Mix a darker hair mixture and apply to areas of the hair, eyes and eyelashes and then add in the necklace. Add shadows to the shirt, using the same darker hair mix. Wet the shirt first and then drop into the darker areas to make the shadows. When this is dry, you can paint in the seam lines.

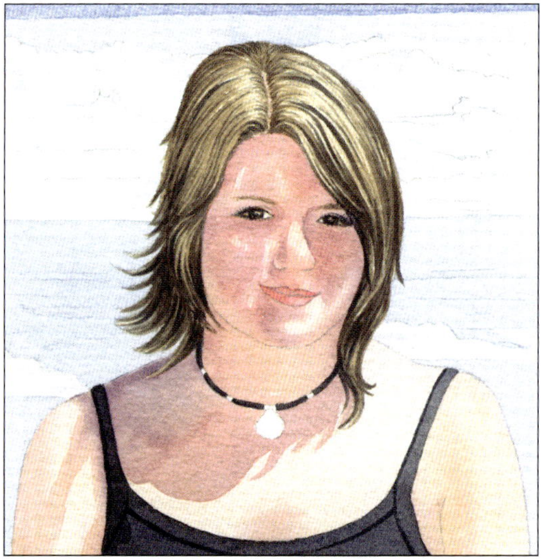

11. With a pale blue add some shadows on the silver pendant and beads. Finally, add some yellow ochre shadows across the water.

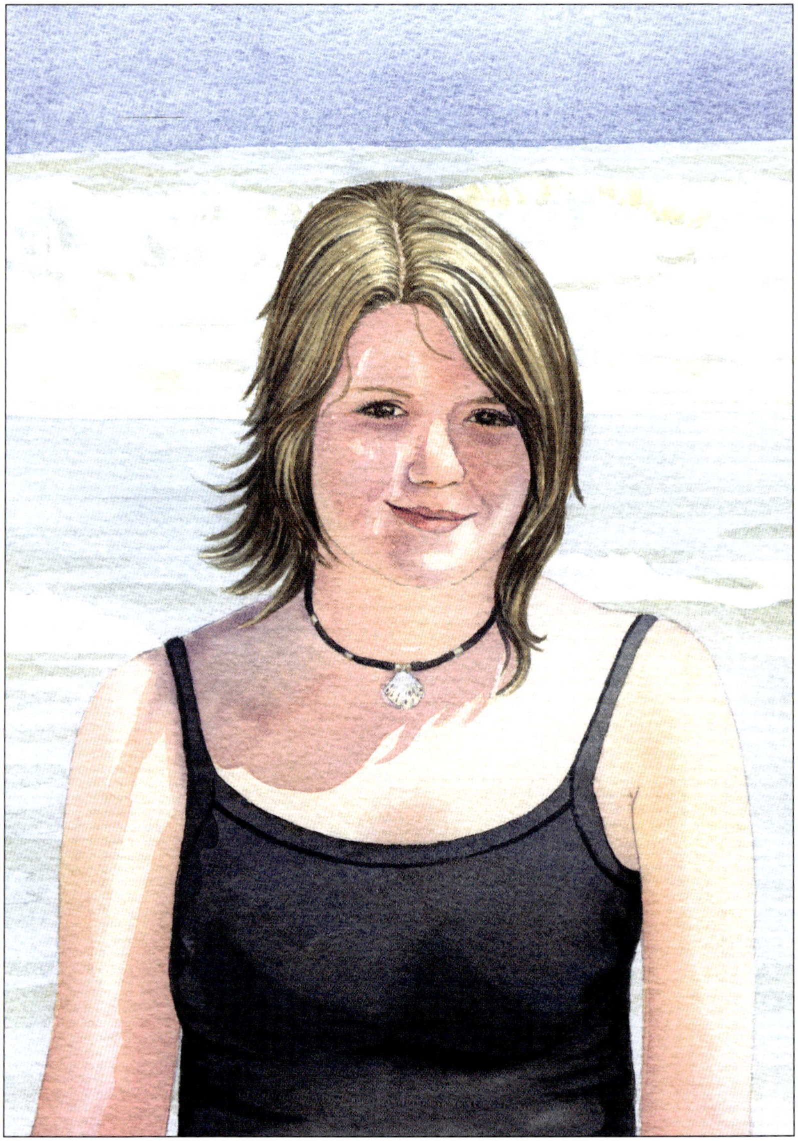

PROJECT TEN: Life Study One

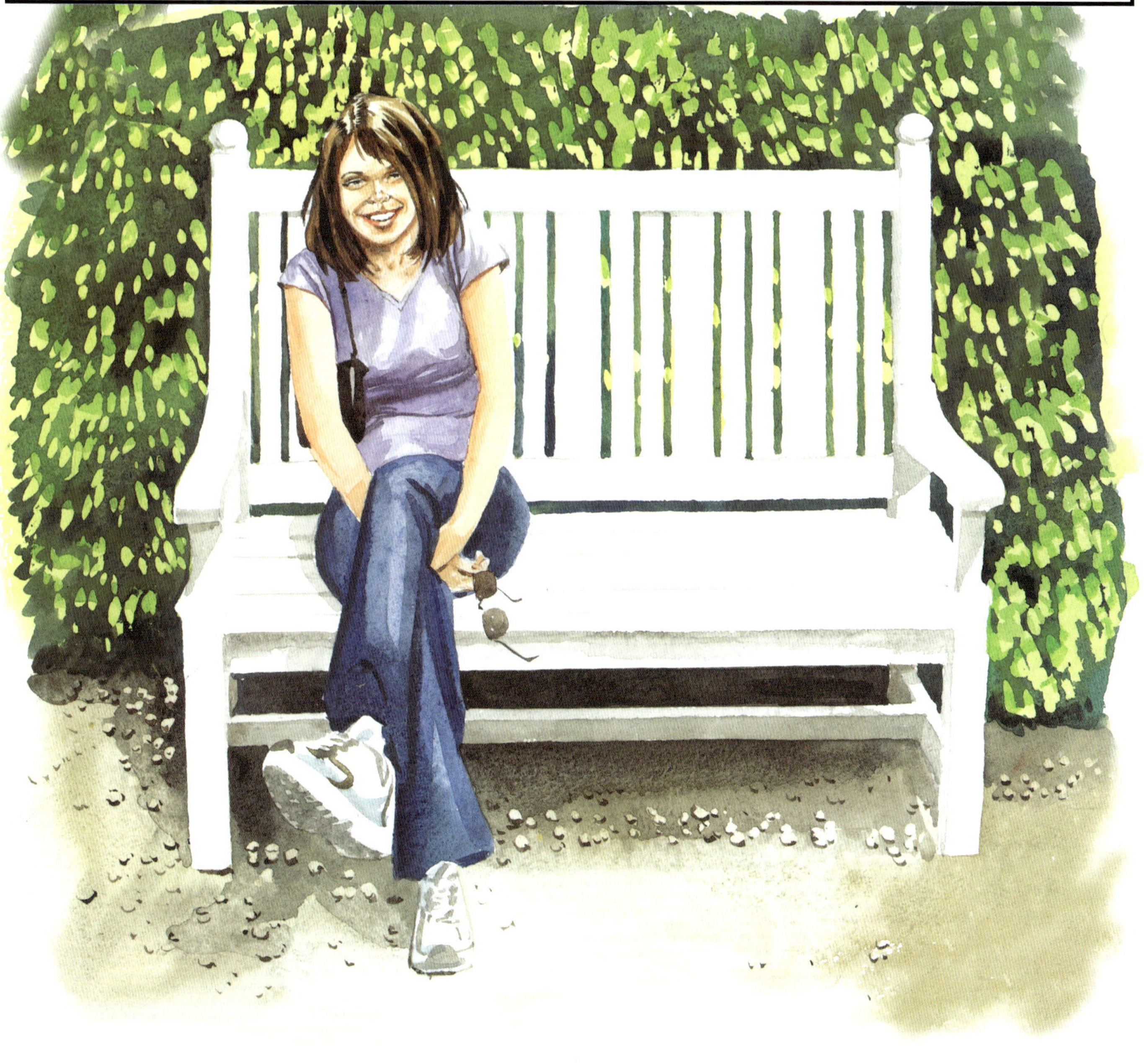

Life Study One

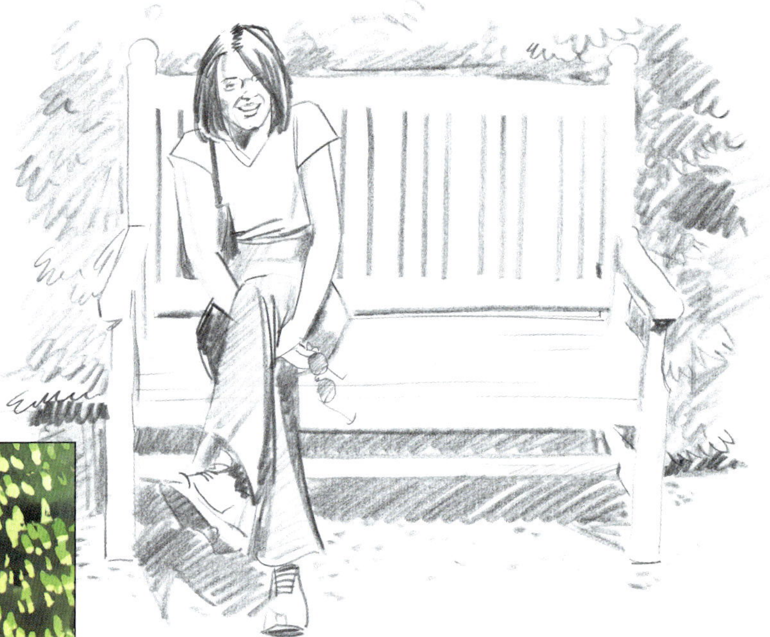

A life study presents a different challenge to other watercolour subjects. However, as long as you are able to master the basics of anatomy, it will not be too daunting a task.

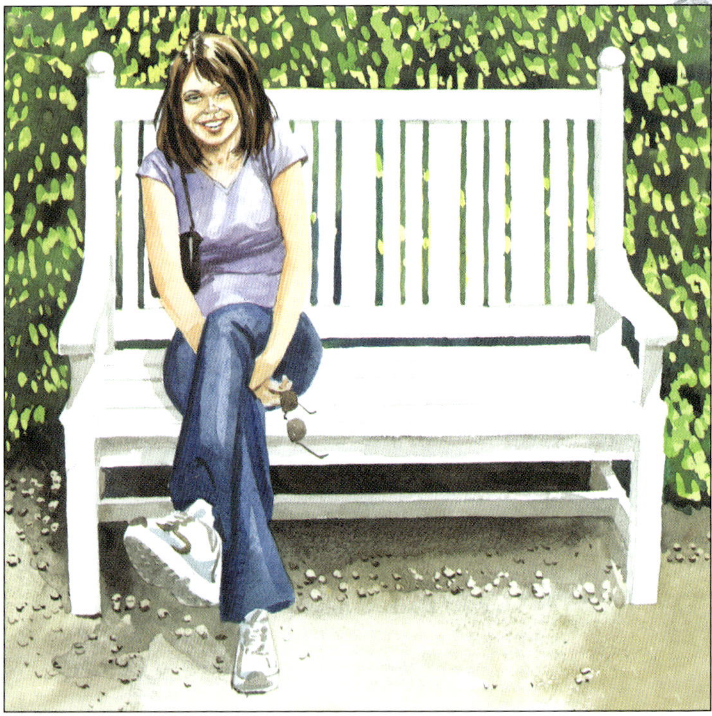

Life Study One

1. Sketch or trace the line drawing on page 94. Use the sketch opposite to help you establish tonal values. Use a pencil for the main shapes, making sure you consider where the light is coming from and where the highlights will fall on your subject.

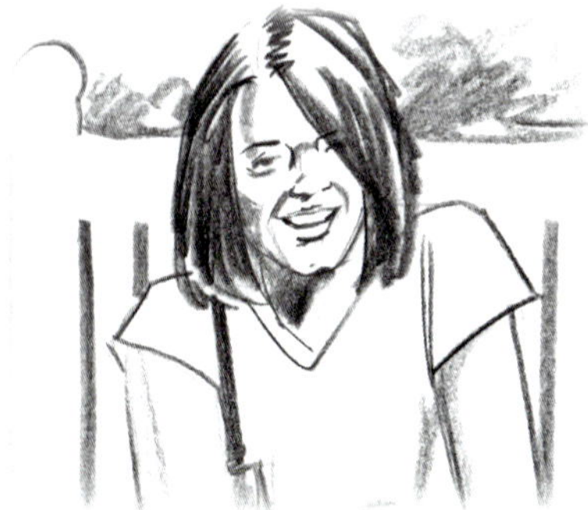

2. Cover the white of the bench with a masking agent. Apply a light greeny-yellow wash to the hedge and allow to dry.

Begin with a light greeny-yellow wash for the hedge.

3. Build up the colours of the hedge using the wet-in-wet technique. Allow to dry before adding concentrated blobs of colour to finish the hedge.

4. Apply a pale wash of creamy brown to the ground and work wet-in-wet to add darker colours. Leave to dry, then add the details of the stones.

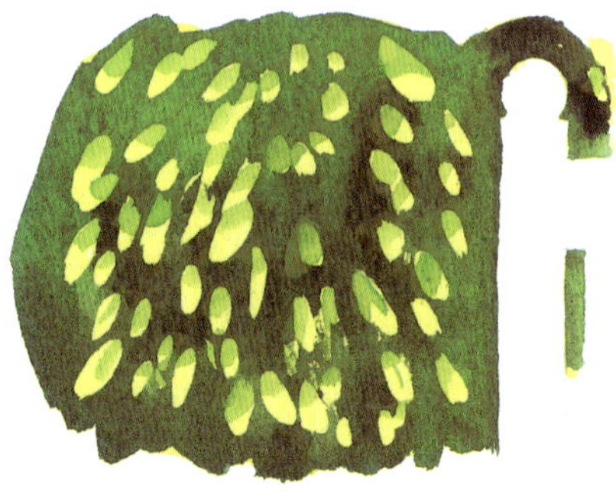

This detail shows the build-up of colours on the hedge.

5. In order to paint the face and arms, begin by adding a very light brown wash on top of your pencil sketch. Then, add more washes of different hues to build up the detail of the skin tone.

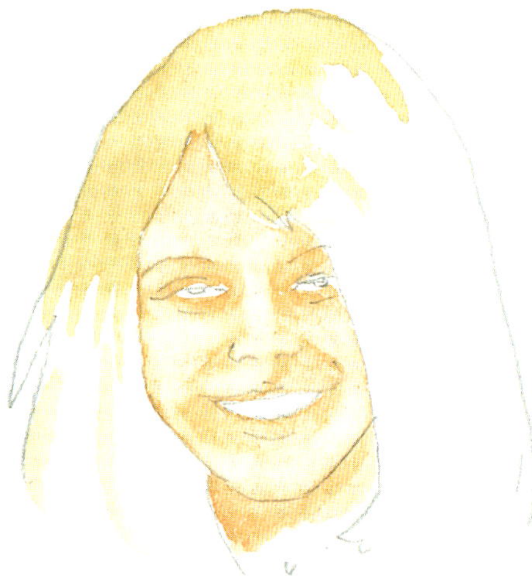

For the face, add a light wash on top of the pencil sketch.

6. Use a fine brush to add the details of the face. Try to be precise when painting eyes, lips and teeth. Use a light brown wash for the hair, adding the darker highlights using the wet-in-wet technique. Do not labour detail or these areas will become muddy.

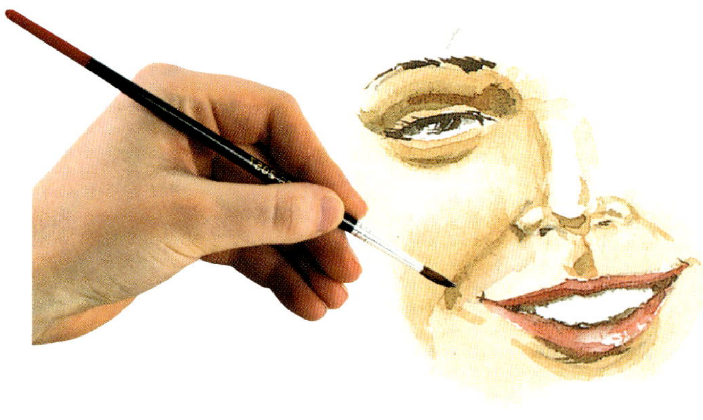

Use a fine brush to add the details of the face.

Life Study One

7. The creases of the clothing should be established in the pencil drawing. It is this sort of attention to detail that makes all the difference when painting life studies, as it makes the subject seem more real. Use a light blue-lilac wash for the T-shirt, washing in darker colour for the shadow.

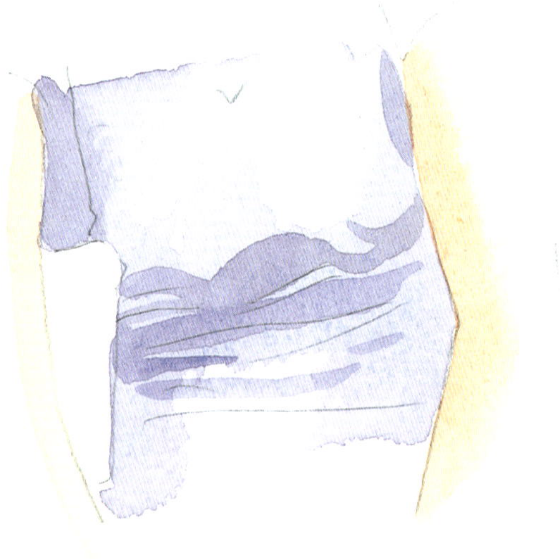

The creases of the clothing should be established in the pencil drawing so that they can be washed over.

8. Use a dark blue wash for the jeans, dabbing out the colour with a paper tissue. When this is dry, add the final parts of the shoes, clothing and dark glasses. When this is complete, work up the details until you are happy that the picture is finished.

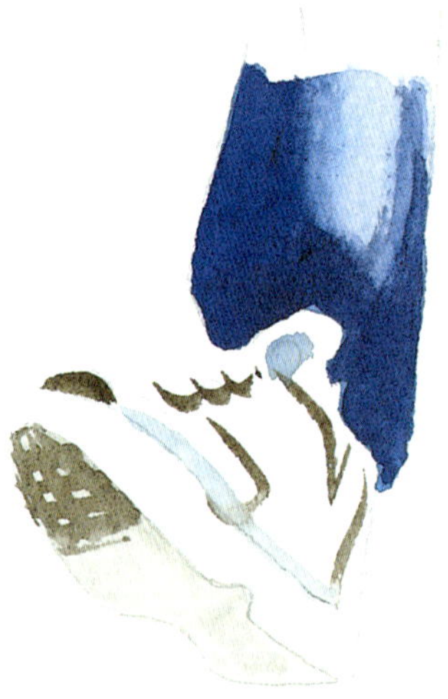

Add the detail of the shoes and clothing last.

PROJECT ELEVEN: Life Study Two

In this composition, the model is sitting with a strong light from the right. This has given a good contrast in light and shade, which helps to define the body shape well.

1. Lightly draw your picture, being careful not to leave unnecessary pencil marks.

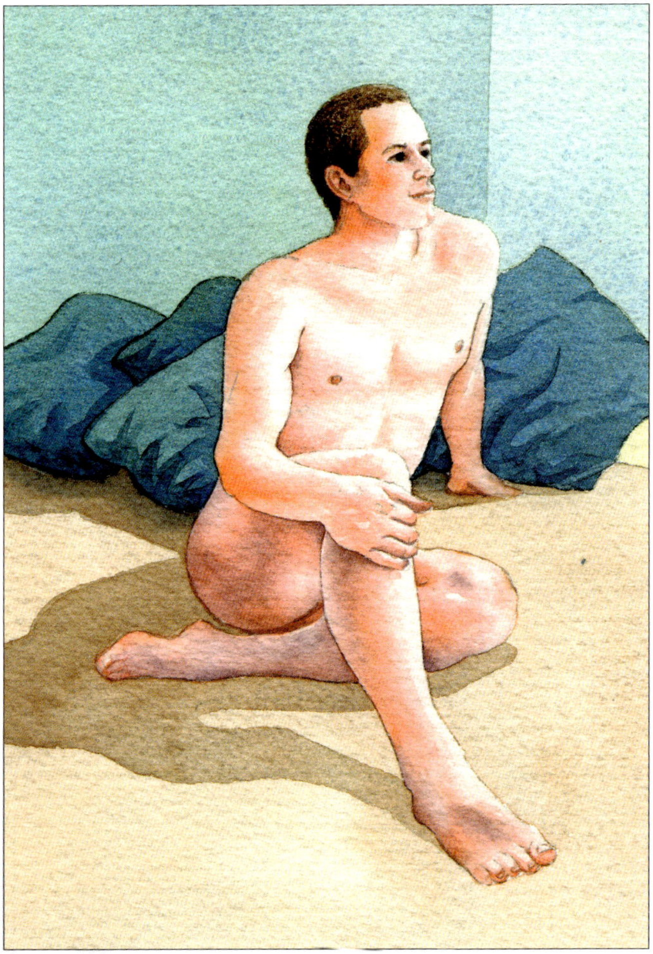

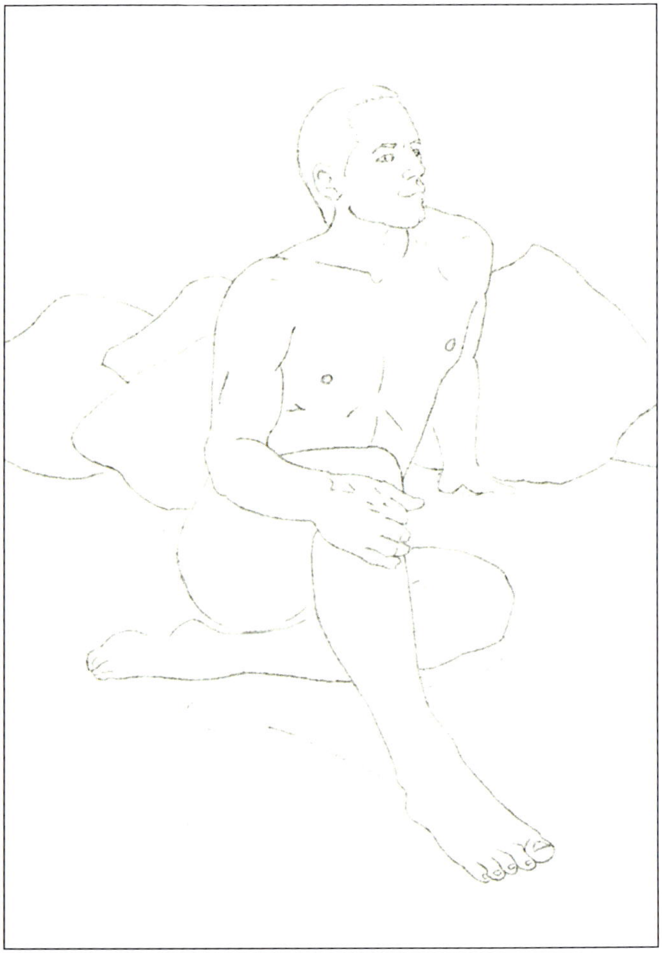

Life Study Two

2. Mix together sap green and ultramarine for the background wall. Wet the paper and apply a simple flat wash across the whole wall, making sure it is even and consistent.

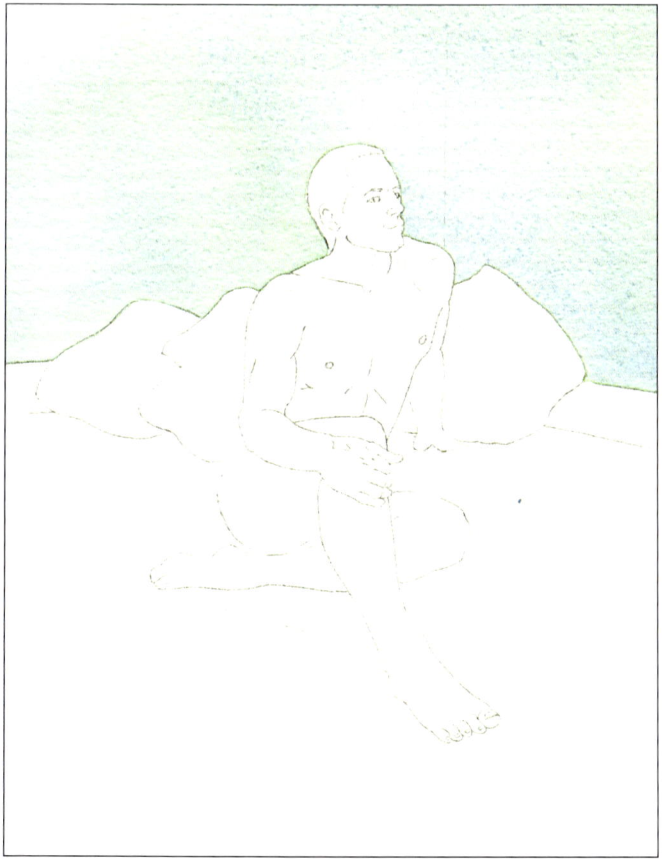

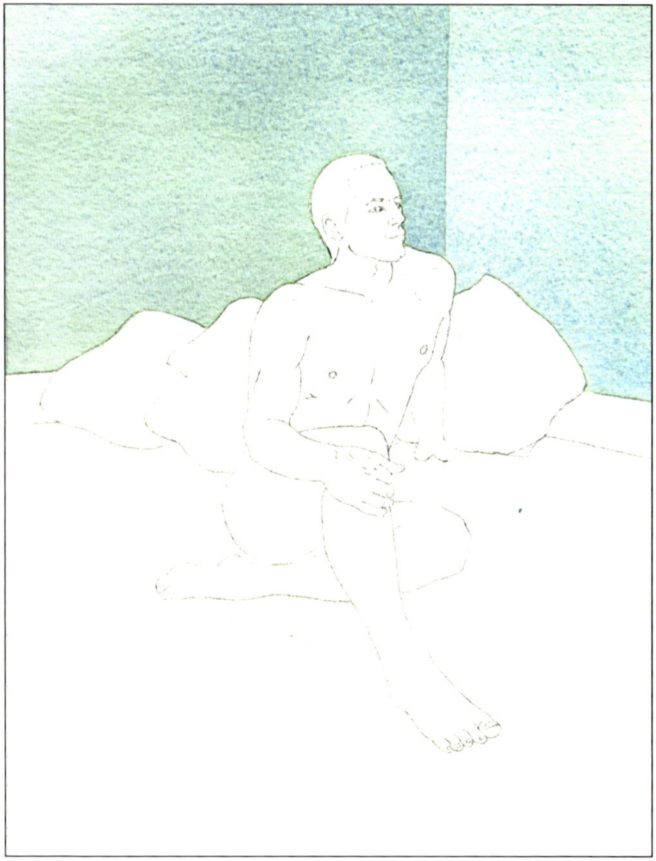

3. With exactly the same mix of sap green and ultramarine, paint over the left side of the wall to create the corner of the room. You will not need to wet the paper for this. In fact, make sure it is dry, or you will not achieve the crisp line that forms the corner.

4. A dilute mixture of burnt sienna with a little ultramarine is used for the carpet. Wet the paper and apply a simple flat wash across the whole of the floor leaving a strip of paper untouched for the skirting board.

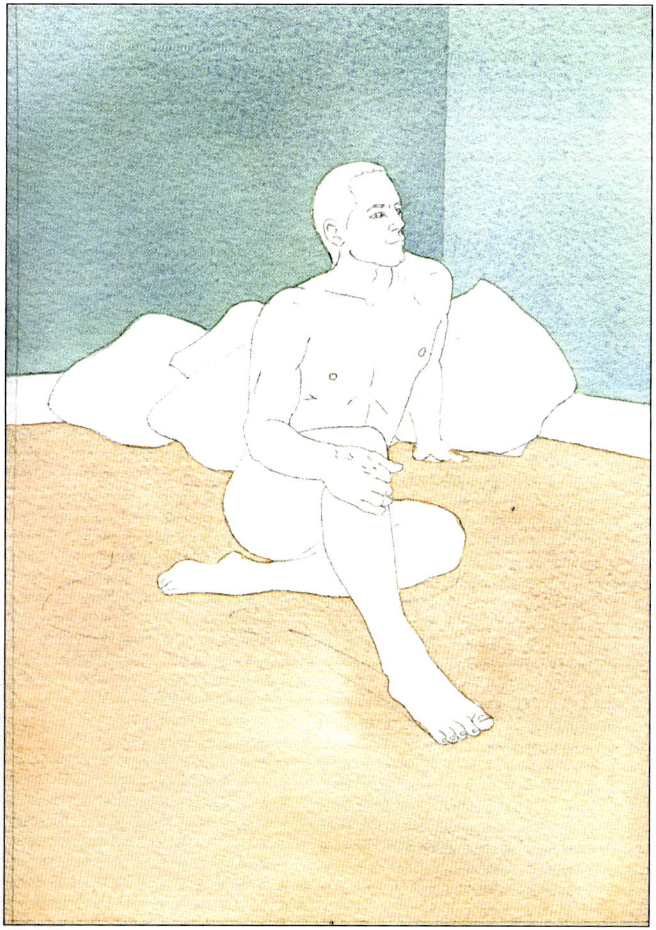

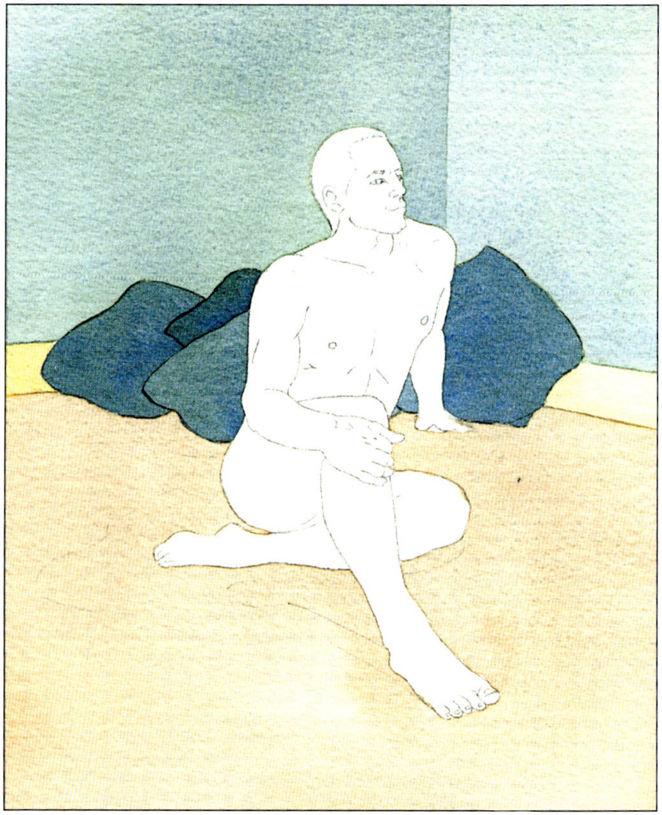

5. Finish off the basic background by painting the base colour of the four cushions and the skirting board. For the cushions, mix ultramarine with sap green to make a deeper, more intense green than the wall. Paint them individually, changing the subtle tones of each, making the one in the foreground the lightest. Then, paint the skirting board with a pale wash of yellow ochre.

6. Mix alizarin crimson with yellow ochre for a basic skin tone and, having moistened the entire body, paint in an even wash. Lift out with a clean, wet brush the very lightest areas that will almost be the paper colour.

7. Apply a base coat of ultramarine and burnt sienna for the hair.

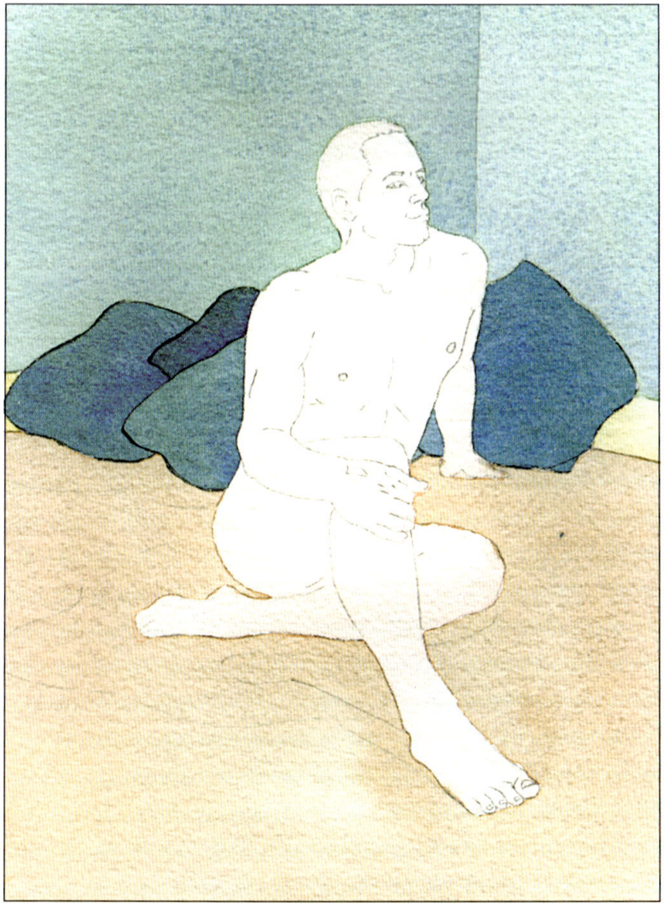

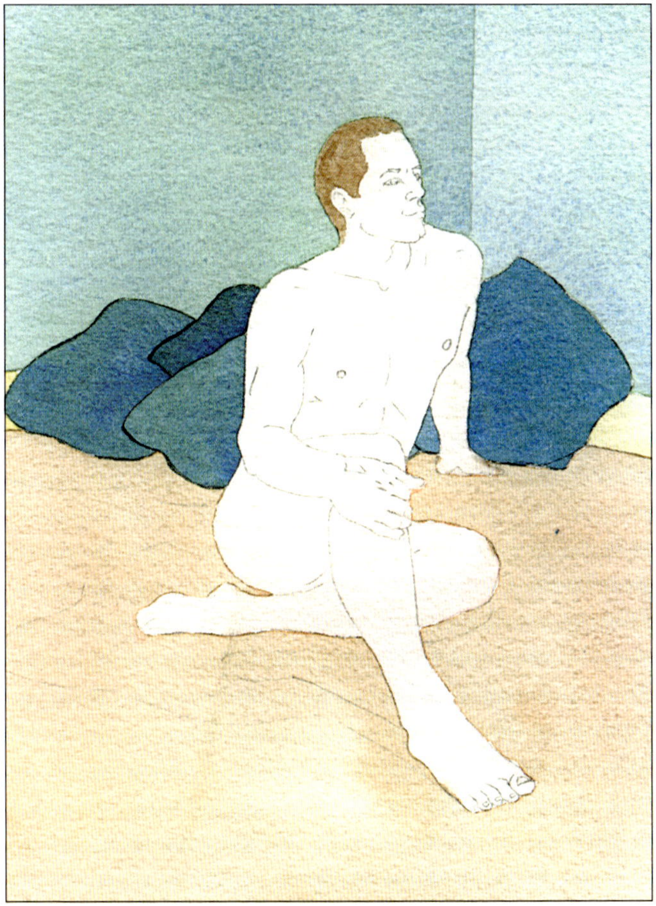

Life Study Two

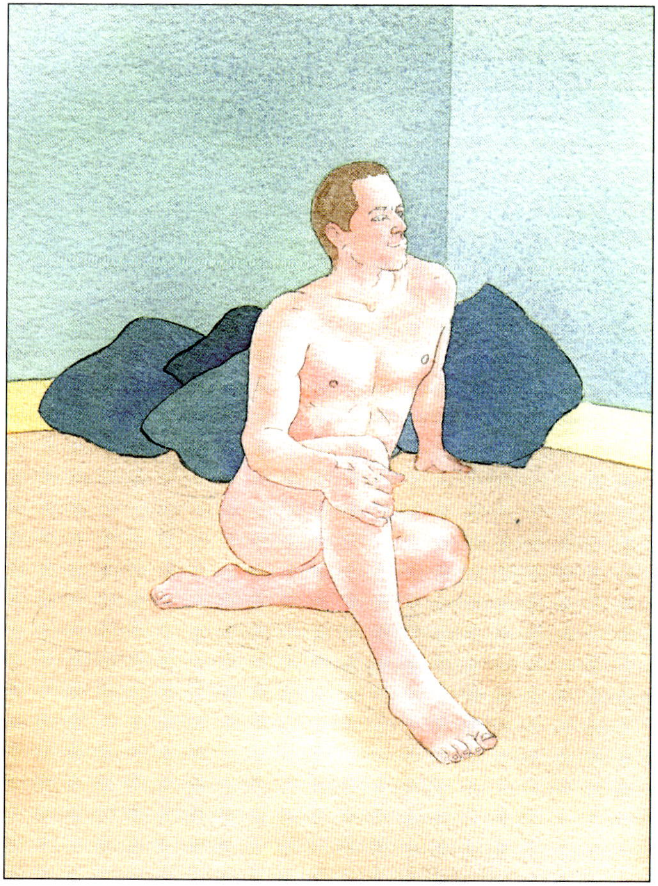

8. Now, bring more life to the figure by adding pinky skin tones, with alizarin crimson, yellow ochre and lemon yellow, remembering to keep the edges soft.

9. Strengthen the darker pinky tones, building and intensifying the colours. Darken the hair with a little more ultramarine and add in the brown of the eyes and eyebrows. Add more intense flesh colours for the lips and shadows around the ears.

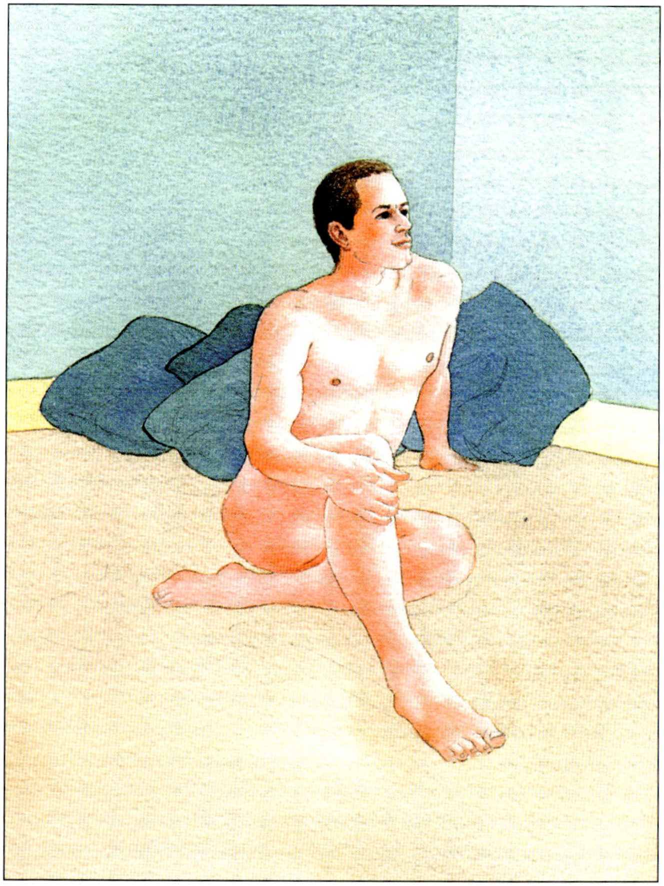

10. Paint the shadows on the carpet using a similar mix of colour as for the carpet, but more intense. Notice how the shadow darkens as it receeds.

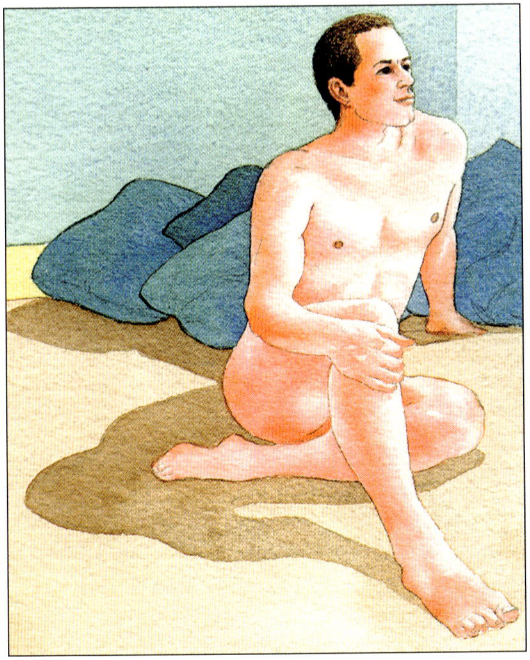

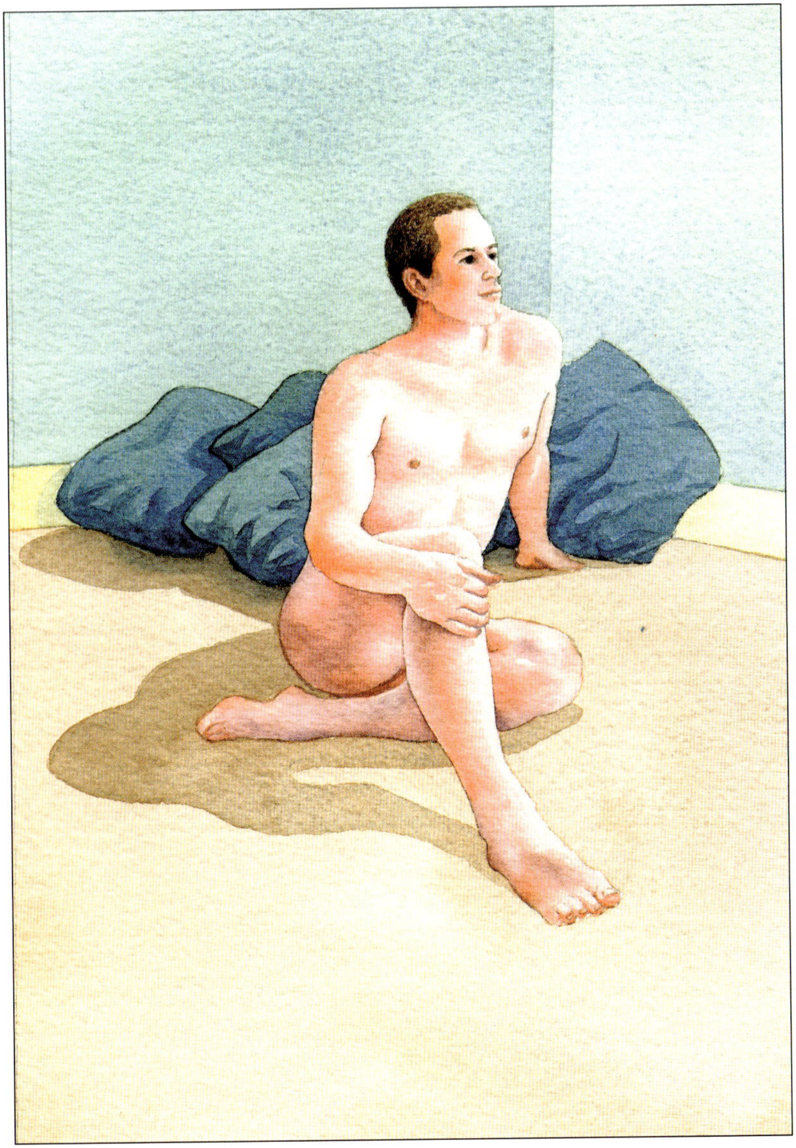

11. Mix sap green and ultramarine for the shadows of the cushions. Then, drop a little of the same colour into the carpet shadow, and soften the edges into the rest of the shadow. Add more ultra-marine to the flesh tint making a purple shade. With this, intensify the form of the body by adding darker shadows.

Drawings to Use

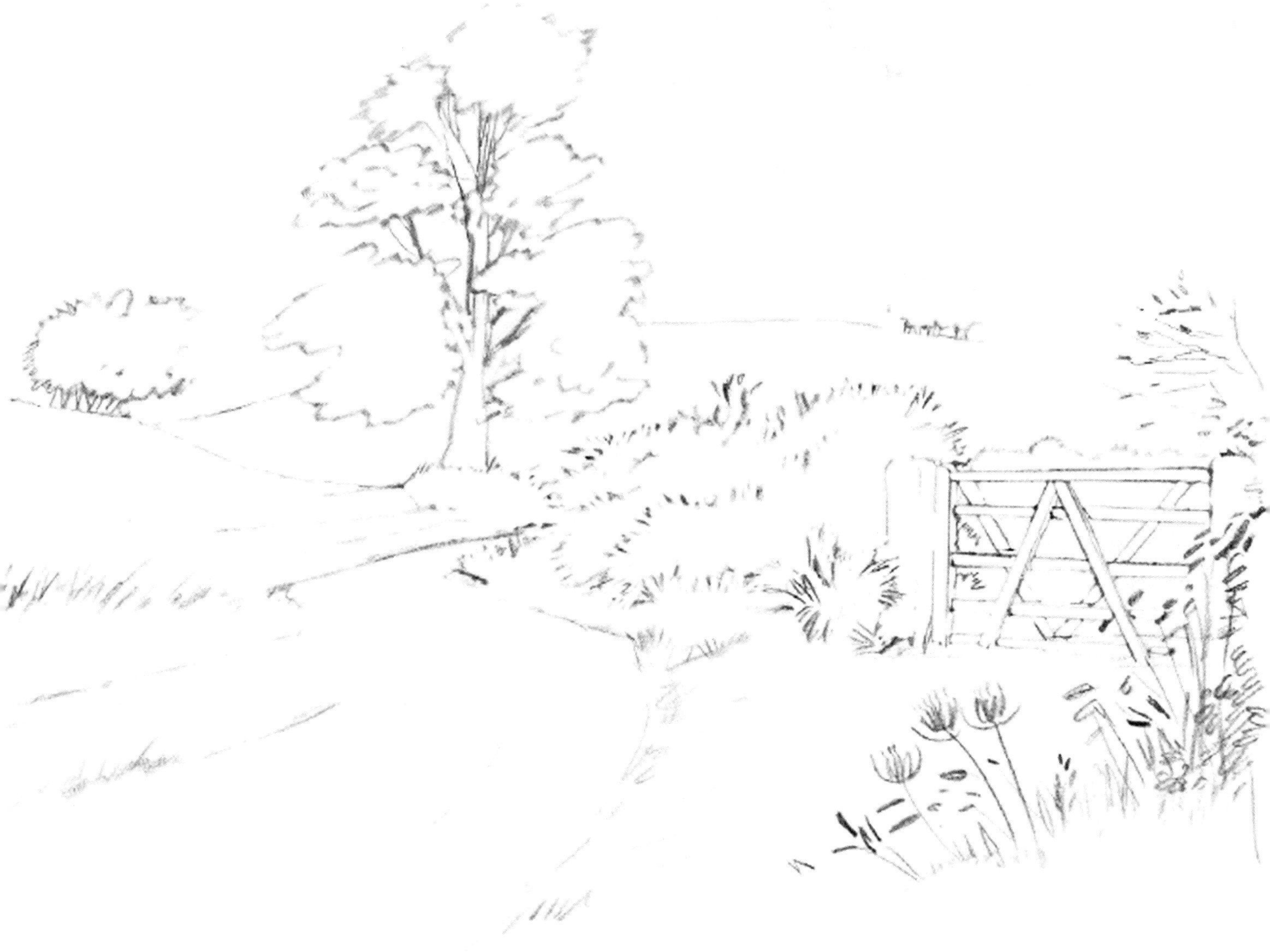

Drawings to Use

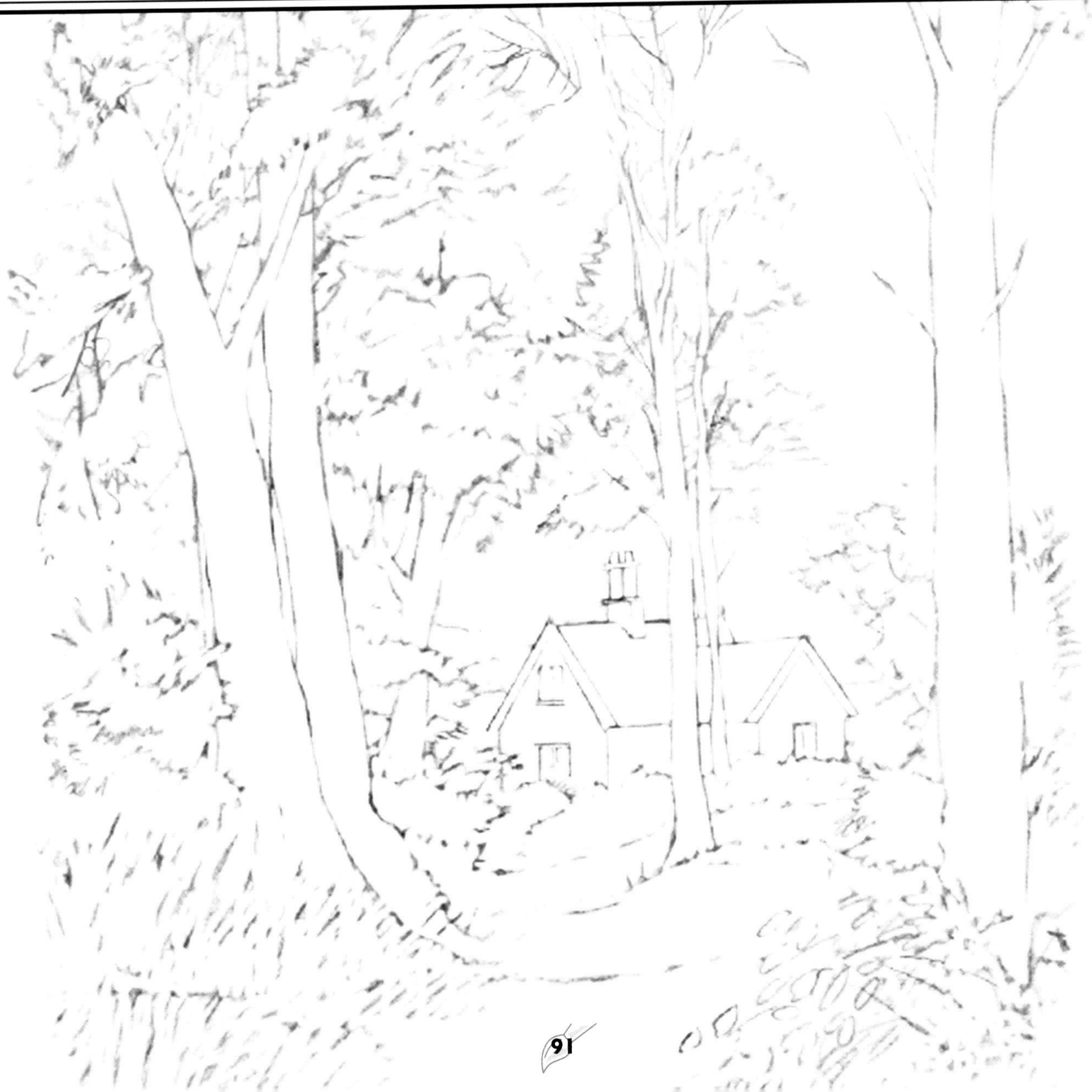

Drawings to Use

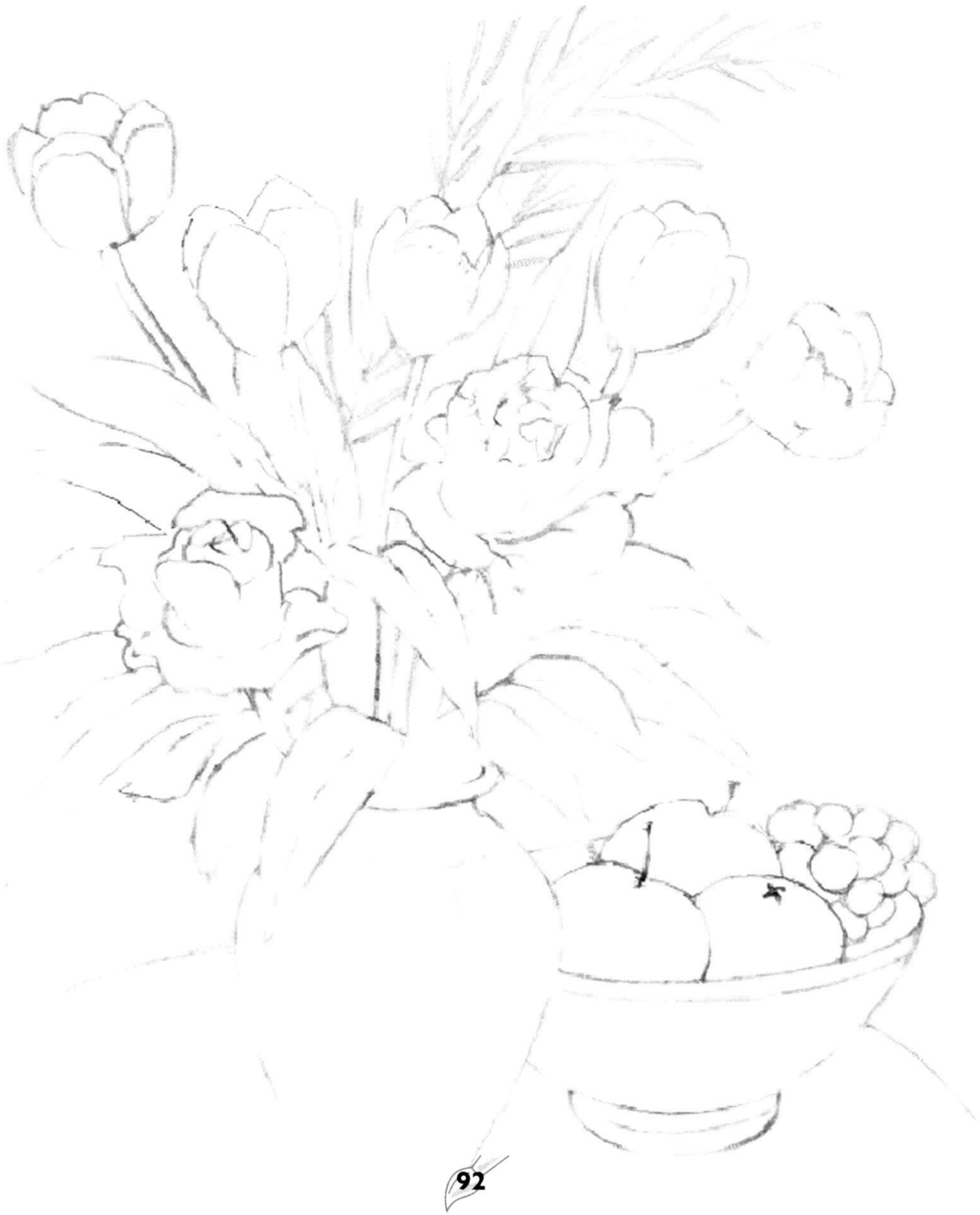

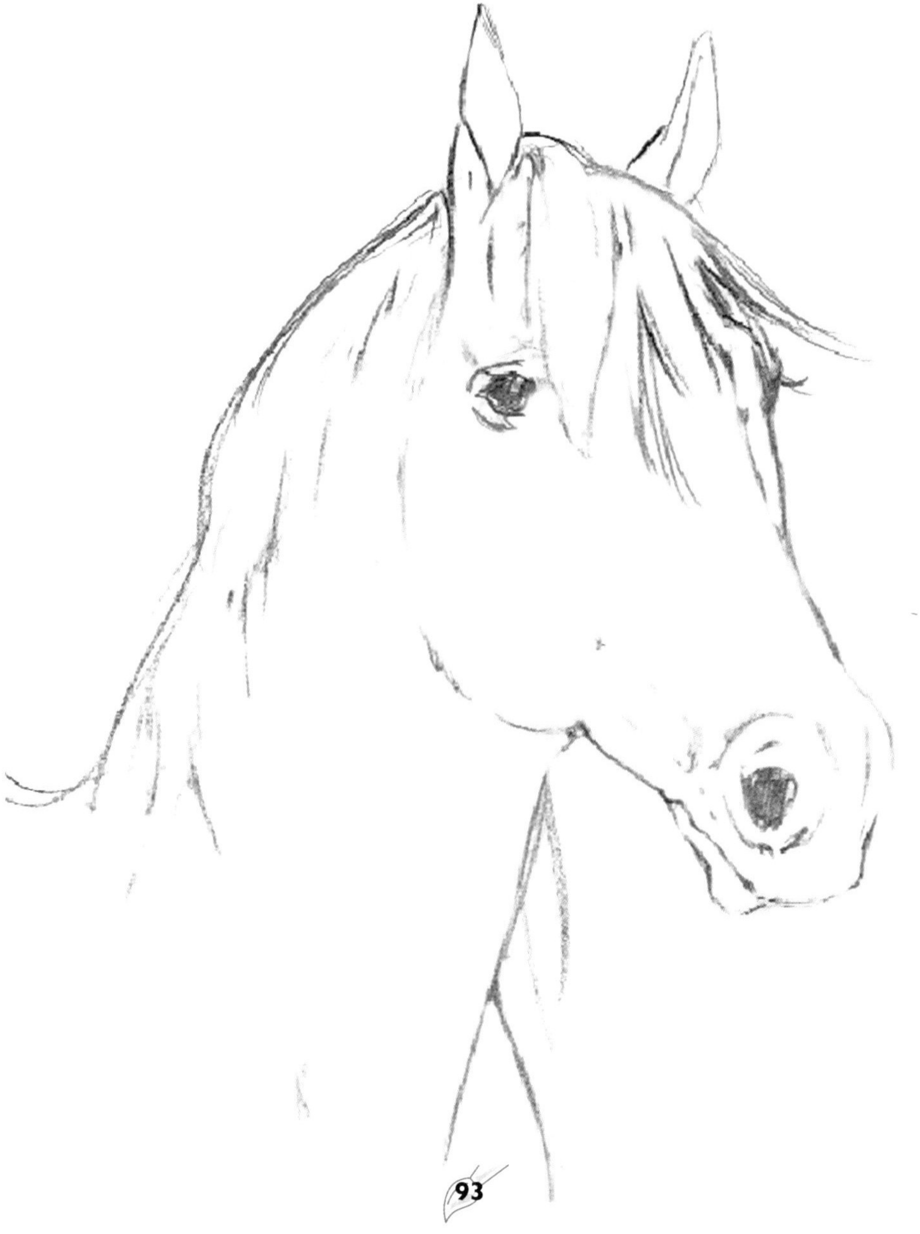

Drawings to Use

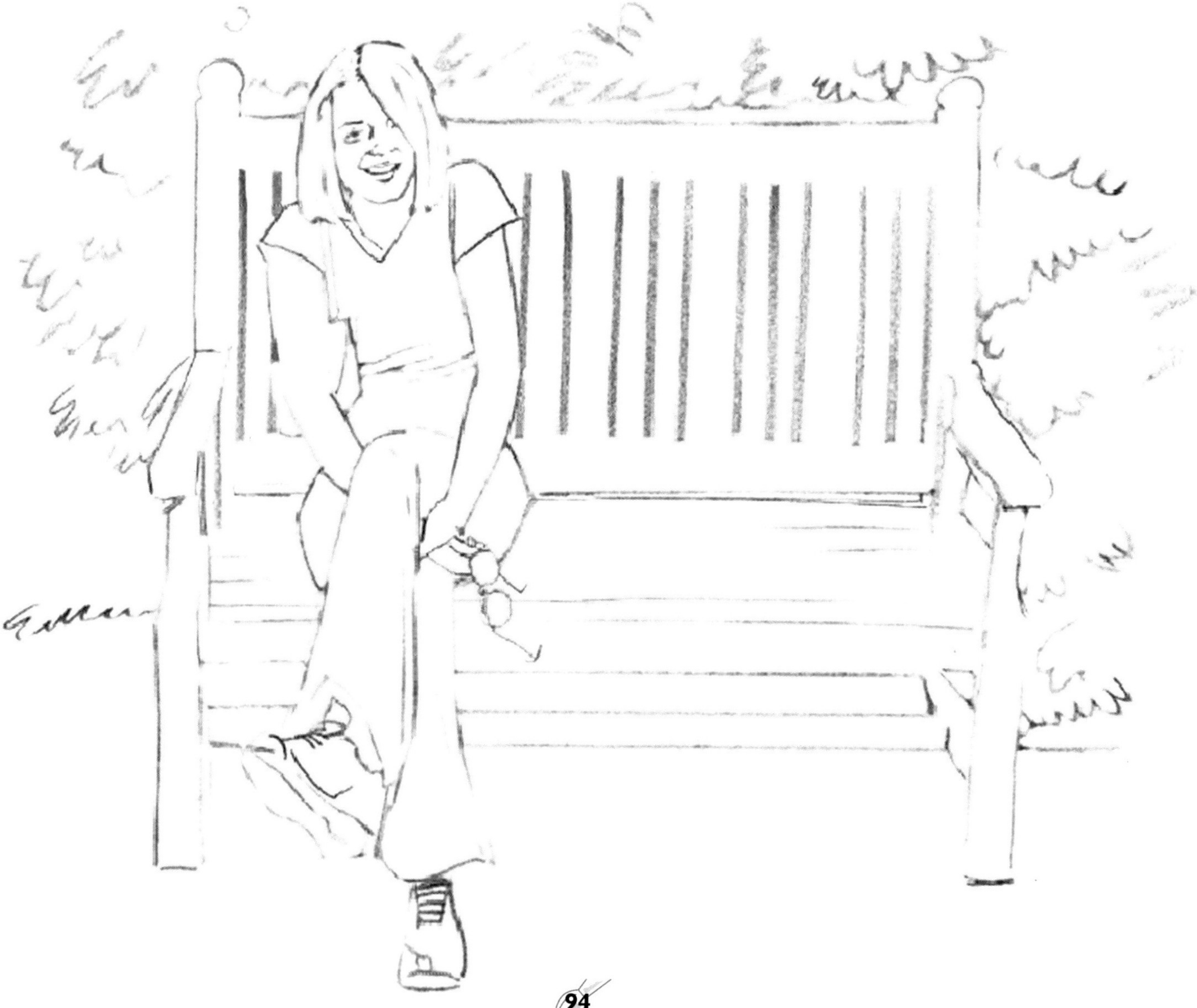

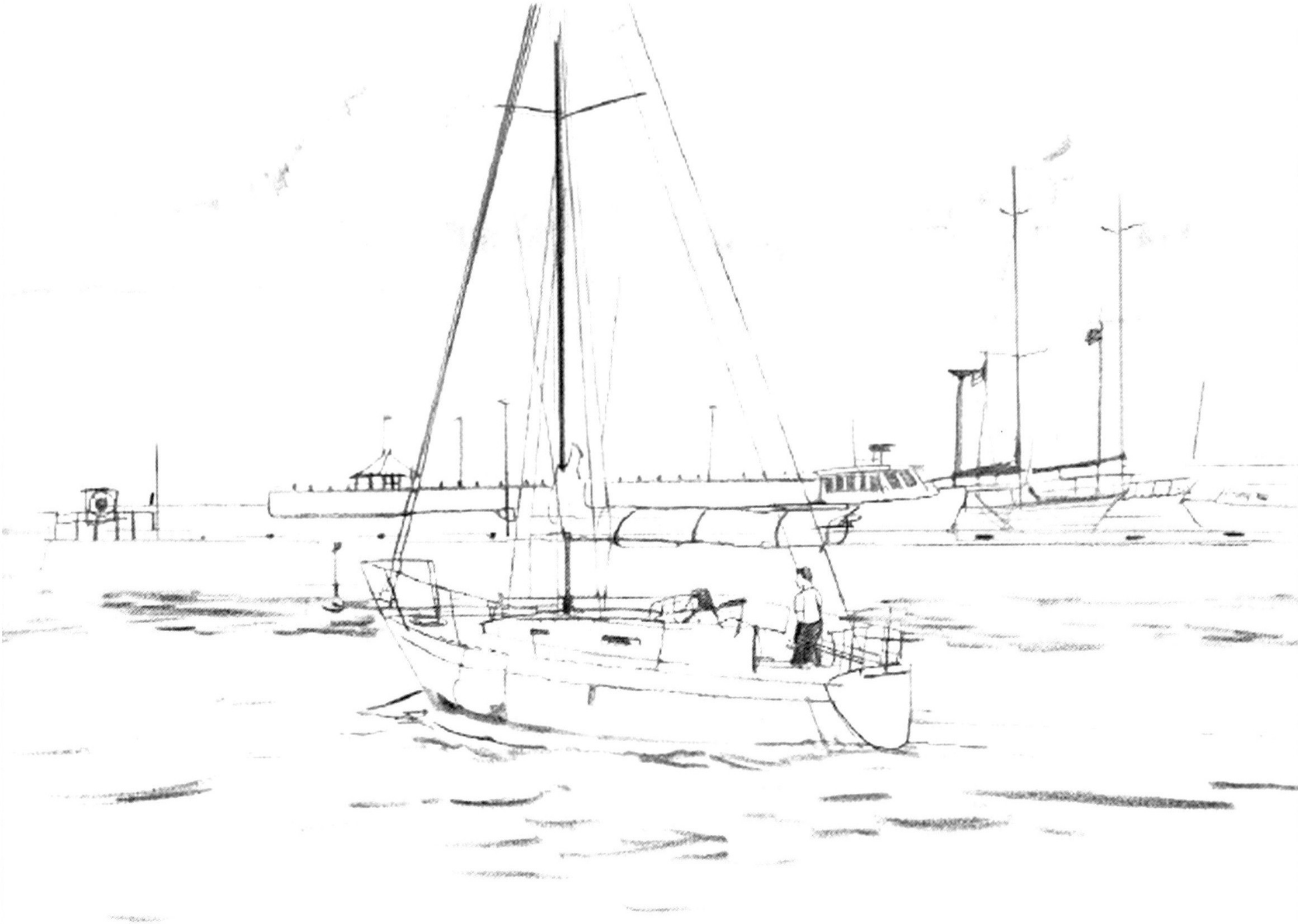

Where to Now?

This book provides you with the basics of how watercolours behave and what makes a good composition – now you just need to go out and put it all into practice.

What do you paint next?
The answer is anything and everything – whatever inspires you or stirs deep emotions. Start looking at the world around you – not just the main images you see, but the contrasts and nuances; that slither of tremendous green light in the corner of a field or an amazing cloud on the horizon.

Always carry a small sketchbook and something to draw with. Often it is a matter of capturing that spontaneous moment or the pose of a figure. Sometimes jotting down words will help revitalise your imagination.

Visit galleries and exhibitions to see other artists' work. Don't worry if they paint in a different medium; they are still capturing the same things and depicting them using light, colour and shade.

Expand your range of materials. Try that better brush and, most of all, try a range of good quality papers; they may be expensive but their price is usually justified. It is surprising what a difference paper can make to a paint's luminosity or the way the surface accepts the colour. The difference is so dramatic that you might want to use different papers for particular paintings.

The best advice is to be bold and brave. Keep experimenting and don't get disheartened. Sometimes artists make huge leaps forward while at other times they seem static, but given time and practice, everyone can progress.

Think about exhibiting with a local group of artists, or a solo exhibition – or just paint for fun. Whatever you do, good luck and happy painting.

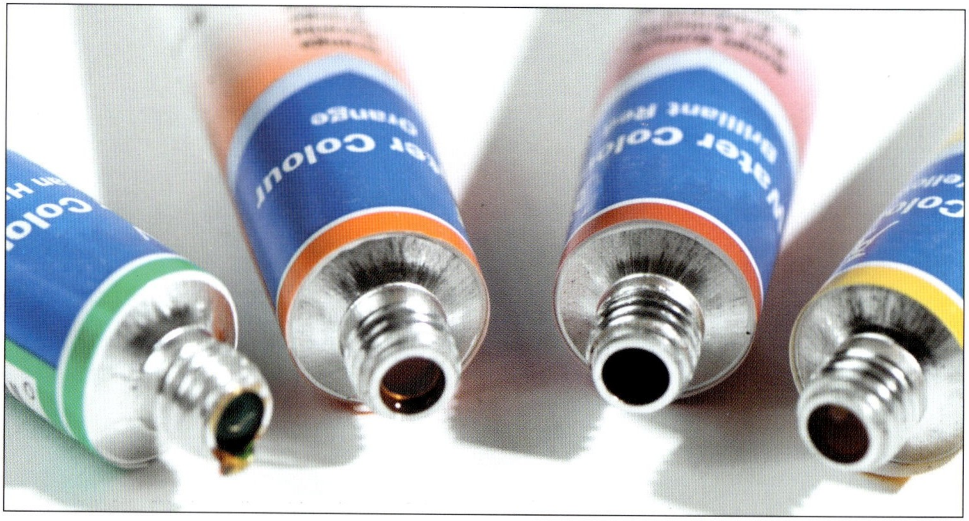